THIRD NEPHI

THE FIFTH GOSPEL

ANDREW C. SKINNER

THIRD NEPHI

THE FIFTH GOSPEL

ANDREW C. SKINNER

CFI
AN IMPRINT OF CEDAR FORT, INC.
SPRINGVILLE, UTAH

ISBN 13: 978-1-59955-979-7

Published by CFI, an imprint of Cedar Fort, Inc., 2373 W. 700 S., Springville, UT 84663
Distributed by Cedar Fort, Inc., www.cedarfort.com

LIBRARY OF CONGRESS CATALOGING-IN-PUBLICATION DATA

Skinner, Andrew C., 1951-, author.
Third Nephi : the fifth gospel / Andrew C. Skinner.
pages cm.
ISBN 978-1-59955-979-7
1. Book of Mormon. Nephi, 3rd. 2. Jesus Christ--In the Book of Mormon. I. Title.

BX8627.S555 2012
289.3'22--dc23

2012007314

Cover design by Rebecca J. Greenwood
Cover design © 2012 by Lyle Mortimer
Edited and typeset by Emily S. Chambers

Printed in the United States of America

10 9 8 7 6 5 4 3 2 1

Printed on acid-free paper

I dedicate this small volume to Janet, Cheryl, Charlie, Stephanie, Lindsey, Connor, Drew, Kelli, Wade, Ammon, Mark, Holly, Bret, and Suzie—all of whom love the Book of Mormon!

Contents

INTRODUCTION
Our Valuable
Fifth Gospel

ON A WINDY DAY IN FEBRUARY 1910, A YOUNG ITALIAN CLERGYMAN, Vincenzo di Francesca, walked down Broadway in New York City. He was on his way to see the pastor of the parish church where he also served. He came upon a trash barrel full of ashes and saw a book lying on top—its pages turning in the stiff wind that was blowing in from the sea. The book was printed in English; its form and binding gave the impression of a religious book. But it had been stripped of its cover and title page. As its pages danced in the wind, Vincenzo hastily glanced over words like Alma, Mosiah, and Isaiah. He wondered if the latter could be the same Isaiah of the Bible.

Vincenzo took the book, completed his errand, and, once he got the book home, began to read it. He became convinced of its truth. He purchased some cotton and denatured alcohol and cleaned its soiled pages. He finished reading the book several hours later, and then he reread it a second, third, and fourth time. After much study, he said he "found it fit to say that the book was a *fifth gospel* of the Redeemer"!¹ He did not find out the source of the book, or which church it was associated with, until two decades later. But he always knew the book was God's work. Many years and much hardship passed, including two world wars, before Brother Vincenzo di Francesca was able to be baptized. But the "fifth gospel" changed his life forever from the moment he first saw it. And as

1

he reflected on his initial encounter with the Book of Mormon on that day in 1910, he could not "escape the feeling that God had been mindful of [his] existence."[2]

Significantly, Brother Francesca felt to call the Book of Mormon a Fifth Gospel of our Savior Jesus Christ. Certainly it is, but the designation "Fifth Gospel" has been most often applied specifically to 3 Nephi, especially by prominent leaders of The Church of Jesus Christ of Latter-day Saints—from Elder B. H. Roberts to President Gordon B. Hinckley. It is rightly called "the fifth Gospel [because] it records the visit of the resurrected Jesus Christ to the more righteous of the Nephites and Lamanites after the land had been cleansed of the wicked. This scripture records both the testimony of the Father and of the Savior, himself."[3]

In 1978, President Hinckley, then known as Elder Hinckley, called 3 Nephi the Fifth Gospel and invited all who did not know of it to seriously investigate it and apply the promise that comes with it—namely, "that if you will read prayerfully you shall know of the truth of this remarkable new witness for Christ."[4] Again in 2004, President Hinckley testified that the Book of Mormon, one of the four "basic cornerstones on which this great latter-day church has been established by the Lord," has at its core "the fifth Gospel, a moving testament of the new world concerning the visit of the resurrected Redeemer on the soil of this hemisphere. . . . It is an unassailable cornerstone of our faith."[5]

In the pages that follow, we shall explore the reasons 3 Nephi may justifiably be called the Fifth Gospel, and why it is so valuable to us. We shall see how 3 Nephi complements and supplements the four biblical Gospels. In a way, it picks up where Matthew, Mark, Luke, and John leave off and strengthens their messages. Even more significant, 3 Nephi emphasizes the most important doctrines, principles, and themes found in the other Gospels. In it we hear the direct voice of the Lord, not filtered through the work of uninspired or careless translators.

Years ago, President N. Eldon Tanner of the LDS Church's First Presidency put it this way:

> I suppose that nowhere in the scriptures do we have a more beautiful or detailed record of God's dealings with man than in the account of this visit as recorded in Third Nephi. . . . Here we can find explanations for many unanswered questions in the Bible. Third Nephi gives us additional information in more detail than the four Gospels in the New Testament, and preserves the doctrines,

teachings, and compassion of the Lord. For this reason there are many who refer to Third Nephi as the 'fifth Gospel.'[6]

Indeed, as the Fifth Gospel, 3 Nephi contains those matters that the Savior himself felt were and are most important to the functioning of his church and absolutely essential for sons and daughters of God to internalize if they want to be exalted. Third Nephi helps us to see with more clarity and precision than the biblical Gospels what "the Gospel" really is—what it is at its heart.

Perhaps most significant, 3 Nephi stands as an independent witness of the linchpin doctrine of the entire Christian faith—the bodily Resurrection of the Lord Jesus Christ. Last but not least, 3 Nephi is a book personally reviewed or edited by the Savior himself. No other Gospel can claim the same editorial authority. Truly, 3 Nephi is worthy of the designation Fifth Gospel—the capstone of all Gospel accounts. It is an anchor to our faith and a crown jewel of inestimable worth in our precious treasury of scripture. It is literally the mind and will of the Father and the Son.

NOTES

1. Vincenzo di Francesca, "I Will Not Burn the Book," *Ensign*, Jan. 1988, 19, emphasis added.

2. Ibid., 18.

3. *New Era*, November 1984, "Q&A: How can I let my nonmember friends know that I'm really a Christian?" online resource.

4. Gordon B. Hinckley, "Be Not Faithless," *Ensign*, May 1978, 61.

5. Gordon B. Hinckley, "The Cornerstones of Our Faith," *Ensign*, Nov. 1984, 51, 52.

6. N. Eldon Tanner, "Christ in America," *Ensign*, May 1975, 34.

1

The Fifth Gospel Testimony of Jesus

LIKE THE GOSPELS OF MATTHEW AND LUKE, 3 NEPHI OPENS WITH A narrative about the birth of Jesus of Nazareth. However, 3 Nephi provides information not found in the New Testament and boasts contents that were reviewed by the Savior himself (3 Nephi 23:7–8). Third Nephi is an important addition to our scriptural understanding of the role and nature of Jesus Christ.

PROPHECIES OF HIS BIRTH

Many years had passed in the Western Hemisphere since the pronounced prophecies of Samuel the Lamanite—which seemed increasingly like false traditions and idle promises to many—and the wicked rose up intending to slay the believers. "Now it came to pass that there was a day set apart by the unbelievers, that all those who believed in those traditions should be put to death except the sign should come to pass, which had been given by Samuel the prophet" (3 Nephi 1:9).

With heavy heart, Nephi importuned the Lord and received a dramatic response:

> And it came to pass that he cried mightily unto the Lord all that
> day; and behold, the voice of the Lord came unto him, saying:

> Lift up your head and be of good cheer; for behold, the time is at hand, and on this night shall the sign be given, and on the morrow come I into the world, to show unto the world that I will fulfil all that which I have caused to be spoken by the mouth of my holy prophets.
>
> Behold, I come unto my own, to fulfil all things which I have made known unto the children of men from the foundation of the world, and to do the will, both of the Father and of the Son—of the Father because of me, and of the Son because of my flesh. And behold, the time is at hand, and this night shall the sign be given. (3 Nephi 1:12–14)

These are important verses doctrinally as well as historically. They affirm that mighty prayer is efficacious and may be measured both in terms of intensity or earnestness *and* in length ("all that day" Nephi cried unto the Lord).

These verses also cause us to reflect on the issue of when the spirit enters the physical body. The following thought is helpful:

> Does the spirit enter the body at the time of conception; at the time of quickening, when the mother first feels signs of life within her; or at the time of physical birth? Can it possibly come and go before the time of birth? . . . We do not know. Such has not been made known to us in the latter days. We do know, however, that the words of God are often spoken through his servants by divine investiture of authority. To Adam the Holy Ghost spoke for and in behalf of the Only Begotten Son (see Moses 5:9). Such may have been the case here: The Spirit may have been commissioned by the Father to speak to Nephi in the first person for Christ, as though Jesus himself were speaking. Another possibility is that an angel, acting by that same investiture of authority, spoke to Nephi the words of Christ (see [Bruce R. McConkie] *Mortal Messiah* 1:349, note 1; compare Revelation 22:6–9). In any event, whether the Lord's words are spoken by himself or by his anointed servants, "it is the same" (D&C 1:38).[1]

In addition, 3 Nephi 1:12–14 confirms that signs and prophecies uttered by prophets will all be fulfilled according to the Lord's timetable. The prophet in this case was the great Samuel the Lamanite. The signs he prophesied that would announce the Savior's birth included great lights in heaven and no darkness on the eve of his nativity, "one day and a night and a day, as if there were no night" (Helaman 14:3–4). The rising of a new star was also promised, and we know that this was fulfilled in the Old World (Matthew 2:1–2; 3 Nephi 1:21).

The obvious theme of additional physical light entering the world with the birth of Jesus Christ has a basis in theology as well as in the laws of the physical universe. The Light of the World, the Great Jehovah, the Anointed One and Son of God, was coming to earth, and the appearance of additional light was literal. As revealed to the Prophet Joseph Smith, the

> light of Christ . . . is in the sun, and the light of the sun, and the power thereof by which it was made.
> As also he is in the moon, and is the light of the moon, and the power thereof by which it was made;
> As also the light of the stars, and the power thereof by which they were made;
> And the earth also, and the power thereof, even the earth upon which you stand.
> And the light which shineth, which giveth you light, is through him who enlighteneth your eyes, which is the same light that quickeneth your understandings;
> Which light proceedeth forth from the presence of God to fill the immensity of space—
> The light which is in all things, which giveth life to all things, which is the law by which all things are governed, even the power of God who sitteth upon his throne, who is in the bosom of eternity, who is in the midst of all things. (D&C 88:7–13)

Third Nephi 1:14 (quoted previously) is perhaps the most significant of all the verses, but it is also the most confusing until one realizes that the premortal Jesus is here speaking in his role as Jehovah. He is telling Nephi that by coming to earth as the mortal Messiah, he will fulfill his other role as the living Christ. Thus, as Father Jehovah (the Israelites knew him as Father), he fulfills his own will by sending himself to earth, and he does the will of the Son when he takes up a physical body to become the earthly Christ. As the Son, it was also his desire to do the will of his actual Father, the mighty Elohim (Abraham 3:27; Moses 4:2). But in 3 Nephi, he was speaking as Father Jehovah before his mortal sojourn.

That Jesus Christ is both the Father and the Son is a doctrine set forth in scripture. To the Brother of Jared, the premortal Christ stated, "Behold, I am Jesus Christ. I am the Father and the Son" (Ether 3:14). In addition, a doctrinal exposition published in 1916 by the First Presidency and Council of the Twelve of The Church of Jesus Christ of Latter-day Saints lays out some of the ways in which Jesus Christ may justly be regarded as the Father.[2]

1. He is the Father as Creator of the heavens and earth. He is Jehovah. Under the direction of God the Father (Elohim), Jesus created worlds without number (Moses 1:32–33). He is the Father of creation. There is one aspect of the creation that he was not responsible for, and that was the creation of spirit children. That act was Elohim's alone.

2. He is the Father of salvation to the faithful. Only through him— his Atonement—may anyone obtain eternal life. He made that possible. The faithful become the "children" of Jesus Christ, his spiritual sons and daughters, born again through him (Mosiah 5:7; 15:10; 27:25).

3. He is the Father by Divine Investiture of Authority. He has power and authority given to him by his actual Father (Elohim) to speak in the first person and act as though he were God the Father. President Joseph Fielding Smith explained the doctrine this way: "The Father has honored Christ by placing his name upon him, so that he can minister in and through that name as though he were the Father; and thus, so far as power and authority are concerned, his words and acts become and are those of the Father."[3] Elder Bruce R. McConkie of the Quorum of the Twelve said this:

> Both the Father and the Son bear the name the *Most High*. (Deut. 32:8–9; Isa. 14:14; Mark 5:7; D&C 36:3; 39:19; 76:57.) This designation connotes a state of supreme exaltation in rank, power, and dignity; it indicates that each of these Gods is God above all. Obviously the Father is the Most High God in the literal sense for he is the God of the Son as well as the God of all men. (John 20:17.) The Son, however, is the Most High God in the sense that by divine investiture of authority, he is endowed with the power and authority of the Father, speaks in his name as though he were the Father, and therefore (having the fullness of the Father) he thinks it "not robbery to be equal with God" (Philip. 2:6.).[4]

In the end, God the Father and his Beloved Son are one, not in personage, but in thoughts, purpose, aims, desires, and divine attributes. What one does the other does or would do; what one thinks the other thinks as well. As the premortal Christ stated, he came unto his own, to fulfill all things which he, as Jehovah, had made known unto the children of men from the foundation of the world (3 Nephi 1:14). He came to his own people, the Jews who rejected him, because it was the will of God the Father (Mosiah 15:7; 3 Nephi 11:11). It thus became his will as well to fulfill all things pertaining to the Father's plan. The other Gospel accounts would later report that Jesus declared that he came into the world to do the will of his Father (Matthew 26:39; Mark 14:36; Luke 22:42; John 4:34; 5:21, 30; 6:38). And the Joseph Smith Translation reports that the last words Jesus uttered before succumbing to death on the Cross was to testify that he *had* fulfilled his Father's will (JST, Matthew 27:50).

Thus, Nephi's description of events in the New World surrounding the Savior's birth in the Old World complements details found in the New Testament Gospels. Third Nephi truly becomes the capstone Gospel, the ultimate "testimony," presenting doctrines and historical fact by quoting Jesus in the first-person rather than merely reporting them in a third-person narrative style.

CRUCIFIXION

After discussing Helaman's prophecies and the Savior's birth, Nephi spent several chapters (3 Nephi 2–7) describing the vicissitudes of Nephite and Lamanite life. This included an increasing wickedness among the people that was driven by oaths and covenants administered by Lucifer himself (3 Nephi 6:28). As the time approached for the rest of Samuel the Lamanite's prophecies to be fulfilled concerning the Savior's death and subsequent Resurrection, secret combinations increased in strength in the New World. Murders on the American continent also increased. We take this as a confirmation of the principle that whenever great righteousness or goodness is about to be manifest, great wickedness instigated by Satan will increase concomitantly. The Son of God was about to be killed, but he was also about to rise from the dead as a glorious Being and appear to the righteous around the world, vanquishing, for a time, the ways of the evil one!

The first intimation of the fulfillment of Samuel's prophecies regarding Christ's death appeared in the thirty-fourth year when a great storm arose, "such an one as never had been known in all the land" (3 Nephi 8:5). Samuel had said:

Yea, at the time that he shall yield up the ghost there shall be thunderings and lightnings for the space of many hours, and the earth shall shake and tremble; and the rocks which are upon the face of this earth, which are both above the earth and beneath, which ye know at this time are solid, or the more part of it is one solid mass, shall be broken up;

Yea, they shall be rent in twain, and shall ever after be found in seams and in cracks, and in broken fragments upon the face of the whole earth, yea, both above the earth and beneath.

And behold, there shall be great tempests, and there shall be many mountains laid low, like unto a valley, and there shall be many places which are now called valleys which shall become mountains, whose height is great.

And many highways shall be broken up, and many cities shall become desolate. (Helaman 14:21–24)

Indeed, all of Samuel's prophecies, revealed to him by an angel (Helaman 14:26), came to pass, as the following chart indicates.

Prophecies Concerning Christ's Death	Recorded Fulfillment
Helaman 14:20, 27—sun darkened, moon and stars refuse to give light for 3 days	3 Nephi 8:19–23
Helaman 14:21, 26—thunder and lightning for many hours	3 Nephi 8:6–7
Helaman 14:21–22—the earth to shake, tremble, and be broken up	3 Nephi 8:12, 17–18
Helaman 14:23—great tempests, mountains laid low and valleys raised	3 Nephi 8:5–6
Helaman 14:24—highways broken up; cities made desolate	3 Nephi 8:8–11, 13
Helaman 14:25—after Jesus's Resurrection, many graves opened and many saints appear unto many people	3 Nephi 23:9–13; Matthew 27:52

Because Jesus Christ was the Light and Life of the World (3 Nephi 11:11) and was in all things and through all things (D&C 88:6–13), when he died the earth convulsed and there was thick darkness for three days (3 Nephi 8:23). The earth is a living entity (Moses 7:48–49), and the light and life of its Creator was leaving. The earth was suffering and mourning this loss. Nephi I, son of Lehi, spoke of this tumult six hundred years before it occurred when he quoted the prophet Zenos:

For thus spake the prophet: The Lord God surely shall visit all the house of Israel at that day, some with his voice, because of their righteousness, unto their great joy and salvation, and others with the thunderings and the lightnings of his power, by tempest, by fire, and by smoke, and vapor of darkness, and by the opening of the earth, and by mountains which shall be carried up.

And all these things must surely come, saith the prophet Zenos. And the rocks of the earth must rend; and because of the groanings of the earth, many of the kings of the isles of the sea shall be wrought upon by the Spirit of God, to exclaim: The God of nature suffers. (1 Nephi 19:11–12)

Third Nephi complements and sometimes expands the accounts of the Savior's crucifixion in the New Testament Gospels. An interesting example is Nephi's description of the thunder, lightning, and quaking of the earth that went on for three hours, as compared to Matthew's, Mark's, and Luke's descriptions of what happened at Golgotha from noon to 3:00 p.m. on the day of Jesus's crucifixion. Third Nephi records:

And there was a great and terrible destruction in the land southward.

But behold, there was a more great and terrible destruction in the land northward; for behold, the whole face of the land was changed, because of the tempest and the whirlwinds, and the thunderings and the lightnings, and the exceedingly great quaking of the whole earth;

And the highways were broken up, and the level roads were spoiled, and many smooth places became rough.

And many great and notable cities were sunk, and many were burned, and many were shaken till the buildings thereof had fallen to the earth, and the inhabitants thereof were slain, and the places were left desolate . . . .

And thus the face of the whole earth became deformed, because of the tempests, and the thunderings, and the lightnings, and the quaking of the earth.

And behold, the rocks were rent in twain; they were broken up upon the face of the whole earth, insomuch that they were found in broken fragments, and in seams and in cracks, upon all the face of the land.

And it came to pass that when the thunderings, and the lightnings, and the storm, and the tempest, and the quakings of the earth did cease—for behold, they did last for about the space of three hours; and it was said by some that the time was greater; nevertheless, all these great and terrible things were done in about the space of three hours—and then behold, there was darkness upon the face of the land. (3 Nephi 8:11–14, 17–19)

Matthew, on the other hand, simply reports: "Now from the sixth hour there was darkness over all the land unto the ninth hour. . . . Jesus, when he had cried again with a loud voice, yielded up the ghost. And, behold, the veil of the temple was rent in twain from the top to the bottom; and the earth did quake, and the rocks rent" (Matthew 27:45, 50–51).

The contrast between 3 Nephi and Matthew is quite dramatic. Third Nephi completes the picture of the great tragedy and catastrophe of the Crucifixion reported in less detail in the other Gospels. Christ hung on the Cross for six hours, from approximately 9:00 a.m. until 3:00 p.m. It was during the last three hours that thick darkness enveloped the land as the agonies of Gethsemane again descended upon him with a fury. Finally, at about 3:00 p.m. the Son of God gave up the ghost, having accomplished all he was asked to do, and death released him from an agony, a torture, a horror so extreme that no other being can even conceive as possible.[5] What happened to our Lord, what he really experienced, during the last three hours upon the Cross we cannot fully know or appreciate. But thanks to 3 Nephi 8, we can better understand the nature and the extent of the geological, geographical, and climatological tumult and destruction that accompanied the Crucifixion as well as the intensity of the darkness that settled in. And thanks to 3 Nephi, it is confirmed that the darkness did cover the whole earth, whereas prior to the coming forth of the Book of Mormon, only Luke indicated that "there was darkness over all the earth until the ninth hour. And the sun was darkened" (Luke 23:44–45).

RELIEF FROM DESTRUCTION

The three days of darkness covering the lands of America seems to correspond to the three-day period that Jesus's lifeless body lay in the borrowed tomb belonging to Joseph of Arimathaea (John 19:38–42). Third Nephi is silent as to details of the Savior's mission in the world of spirits. But it certainly tells us much about the suffering of people in the New World who remained alive amidst a broken landscape. We read:

And it came to pass that it did last for the space of three days that there was no light seen; and there was great mourning and howling and weeping among all the people continually; yea, great were the groanings of the people, because of the darkness and the great destruction which had come upon them.

And in another place they were heard to cry and mourn, saying: O that we had repented before this great and terrible day, and had not killed and stoned the prophets, and cast them out; then would our mothers and our fair daughters, and our children have been spared, and not have been buried up in that great city Moronihah. And thus were the howlings of the people great and terrible. (3 Nephi 8:23, 25)

Out of the midst of darkness a voice was heard by all the surviving inhabitants of the land, claiming responsibility for all the destruction that had occurred, including the deaths of many people (3 Nephi 9:1–12). The speaker then identified himself as the very Messiah who they had rejected or ignored. We can only imagine the shock and awe that must have reverberated through the population as they heard the words:

O all ye that are spared because ye were more righteous than they, will ye not now return unto me, and repent of your sins, and be converted, that I may heal you?

Yea, verily I say unto you, if ye will come unto me ye shall have eternal life. Behold, mine arm of mercy is extended towards you, and whosoever will come, him will I receive; and blessed are those who come unto me.

Behold, I am Jesus Christ the Son of God. I created the heavens and the earth, and all things that in them are. I was with the Father from the beginning. I am in the Father, and the Father in me; and in me hath the Father glorified his name.

I came unto my own, and my own received me not. And the scriptures concerning my coming are fulfilled. (3 Nephi 9:13–16)

It is telling, I think, that Jesus chose to offer to "heal" the suffering population. Jesus Christ is the Great Healer. The New Testament Gospels and 3 Nephi are filled with examples of Jesus performing miracles of physical healing. However, the Savior's greatest healing power comes from his atoning sacrifice. No doubt some people were injured physically, but all were sick spiritually. They were like those in Jerusalem who had "received him not"—rejected or ignored him. These needed his help most of all. Others have noted that the Savior's offer to heal the remnant of the Nephites and Lamanites was spiritual as well as physical:

Through faith in Him and repentance, sick, sin-ridden, souls are healed by the Great Physician as much so as bodies were in the cleansing of lepers. The Savior's healing declaration, "Be thou clean" (see Matthew 8:2–3), is a literal promise to the faithful and repentant. It may be that all of the miraculous healings performed by Jesus were but tangible symbols of the greatest healing that he alone could perform—the healing of sick spirits and the cleansing of sin-stained souls. "The greatest miracles I see today," declared President Harold B. Lee, "are not necessarily the healing of sick bodies, but the greatest miracles I see are the healing of sick souls, those who are sick in soul and spirit and are downhearted and distraught, on the verge of nervous breakdowns" (Conference Report, April 1973, p. 178).[6]

After he called for the American Israelites to repent, the Savior not only declared the Law of Moses to be fulfilled (3 Nephi 9:17) but also instituted a new order of worship and sacrifice. He declared:

And ye shall offer up unto me no more the shedding of blood; yea, your sacrifices and your burnt offerings shall be done away, for I will accept none of your sacrifices and your burnt offerings. And ye shall offer for a sacrifice unto me a broken heart and a contrite spirit. And whoso cometh unto me with a broken heart and a contrite spirit, him will I baptize with fire and with the Holy Ghost, even as the Lamanites, because of their faith in me at the time of their conversion, were baptized with fire and with the Holy Ghost, and they knew it not. (3 Nephi 9:19–20)

What is truly stunning here is the content and structure of the new order of obedience and sacrifice. The old system of animal sacrifice was fulfilled and not to be carried out any longer. He now required of his followers an offering of a broken heart and contrite spirit—the very conditions he himself experienced in Gethsemane and at Golgotha. From then on, disciples were to offer what God offered! How so?

It is well known that some profound gospel thinkers believe Jesus died of a broken heart on the Cross. Elder James E. Talmage, for one, stated:

While, as stated in the text, the yielding up of life was voluntary on the part of Jesus Christ, for He had life in Himself and no man could take His life except as He willed to allow it to be taken, (John 1:4; 5:26; 10:15–18) there was of necessity a direct physical cause of dissolution. . . . The crucified sometimes lived for days upon the cross, and death resulted, not from the infliction of mortal wounds, but from internal congestion, inflammations, organic disturbances, and consequent exhaustion of vital energy. Jesus, though weakened by long torture during the preceding night and early morning, by the shock of the crucifixion itself, as also by intense mental agony, and particularly through spiritual suffering such as no other man has ever endured, manifested surprising vigor, both of mind and body, to the last. The strong, loud utterance, immediately following which He bowed His head and "gave up the ghost," when considered in connection with other recorded details, points to a physical rupture of the heart as the direct cause of death. If the soldier's spear was thrust into the left side of the Lord's body and actually penetrated the heart, the outrush of "blood and water" observed by John is further evidence of a cardiac rupture; for it is known that in the rare instances of death resulting from a breaking of any part of the wall of the heart, blood accumulates within the pericardium, and there undergoes a change by which the corpuscles separate as a partially clotted mass from the almost colorless, watery serum. . . . Great mental stress, poignant emotion either of grief or joy, and intense spiritual struggle are among the recognized causes of heart rupture.

The present writer believes that the Lord Jesus died of a broken heart. The psalmist sang in dolorous measure according to his inspired prevision of the Lord's passion: "Reproach hath broken my heart; and I am full of heaviness: and I looked for some to take pity, but there was none; and for comforters, but I found none. They gave me also gall for my meat; and in my thirst they gave me vinegar to drink." (Psalm 69:20, 21; see also 22:14.)[7]

Thus, when Jesus's disciples offer up a broken heart, they imitate their Master in a profound way. They *choose* to become like him.

Jesus also commanded the people in the New World to offer a contrite spirit. This too is rooted in his own atoning experience, which he had just completed. The word "contrite" literally means "crushed." Jesus was crushed for us in Gethsemane as the weight of our sins, sorrows, and suffering caused him to feel heavy, weighed down, and sorrowful even unto death (Mark 14:33–34). As disciples of Christ offer a contrite spirit as a personal sacrifice to honor him, they again imitate the Savior in very deed. As they realize their nothingness *without* him and their total dependence *upon* him, they act in different ways than before, and they begin to replicate the results of his personal sacrifice. They forge an immutable bond with their Redeemer.

BITTER CUP EMPHASIZED

The record does not tell us exactly how long after the voice was heard
that the marvelous, awe-inspiring, physical appearance of our resurrected
Lord took place. The text only says,

> And it came to pass that in the ending of the thirty and fourth
> year, behold, I will show unto you that the people of Nephi who
> were spared, and also those who had been called Lamanites, who
> had been spared, did have great favors shown unto them, and great
> blessings poured out upon their heads, insomuch that soon after the
> ascension of Christ into heaven he did truly manifest himself unto
> them—Showing his body unto them, and ministering unto them;
> and an account of his ministry shall be given hereafter. Therefore for
> this time I make an end of my sayings. (3 Nephi 10:18–19)

The description of his appearance to twenty-five hundred souls at the
temple in the land Bountiful is well known and striking (3 Nephi 11).
Surely it is the crowning event of Book of Mormon history and parallels the appearance of the Father and the Son to Joseph Smith in the
Sacred Grove. The Father's introduction of his Beloved Son at the temple
in the land Bountiful is impressive because it is only one of a handful of
occasions when the Father's presence and personal testimony have been
recorded in scripture.

To me, however, the most significant thing in 3 Nephi is the way Jesus
chose to introduce himself: "And it came to pass that he stretched forth
his hand and spake unto the people, saying: Behold, I am Jesus Christ,
whom the prophets testified shall come into the world. And behold, I am
the light and the life of the world; and I have drunk out of that bitter cup
which the Father hath given me, and have glorified the Father in taking
upon me the sins of the world, in the which I have suffered the will of the
Father in all things from the beginning" (3 Nephi 11:9–11). Of all the
things he could have said, it was the bitter cup and suffering the will of
the Father that he emphasized. Careful reflection upon "the bitter cup"
immediately points us to the horror and suffering in Gethsemane. It is
almost as though that experience became the defining memory of mortality for the Savior.

When in Gethsemane and the spiritual onslaught that constituted
the bitter cup began to engulf the Savior, he pled with his Father that it
be removed (Matthew 26:39; Mark 14:36; Luke 22:42). After all, as John

indicates, the bitter cup was the Father's doing: "Then said Jesus unto Peter, . . . the cup which my Father hath given me, shall I not drink it?" (John 18:11).

Matthew tells us that in Gethsemane the bitter cup became so intense that Jesus pled at least three times for its removal:

> And he went a little further, and fell on his face, and prayed, saying, O my Father, if it be possible, let this cup pass from me: nevertheless not as I will, but as thou wilt.
>
> And he cometh unto the disciples, and findeth them asleep, and saith unto Peter, What, could ye not watch with me one hour?
>
> Watch and pray, that ye enter not into temptation: the spirit indeed is willing, but the flesh is weak.
>
> He went away again the second time, and prayed, saying, O my Father, if this cup may not pass away from me, except I drink it, thy will be done.
>
> And he came and found them asleep again: for their eyes were heavy.
>
> And he left them, and went away again, and prayed the third time, saying the same words. (Matthew 26:39–44)

The intensity of the bitter cup remained so fresh on the Savior's mind, perhaps even increasing in his memory, that eighteen hundred years later he used it to define godly suffering to saints of this dispensation. He said:

> For behold, I, God, have suffered these things for all, that they might not suffer if they would repent;
>
> But if they would not repent they must suffer even as I;
>
> Which suffering caused myself, even God, the greatest of all, to tremble because of pain, and to bleed at every pore, and to suffer both body and spirit—and would that I might not drink the bitter cup, and shrink—
>
> Nevertheless, glory be to the Father, and I partook and finished my preparations unto the children of men.
>
> Wherefore, I command you again to repent, lest I humble you with my almighty power; and that you confess your sins, lest you suffer these punishments of which I have spoken, of which in the smallest, yea, even in the least degree you have tasted at the time I withdrew my Spirit. (D&C 19:16–20)

It has always been a curiosity to me that a dash appears at the end of verse eighteen, almost as though Joseph Smith is trying to tell modern readers that the suffering was so great for the Savior in that moment, and he remembered it so exquisitely that he simply could not go on describing it. In other words, in the Savior's perfect memory, it was as though he was actually reliving in the present the experience of the past.

When I reflect on the bitter cup, I do not doubt the assessment of President Joseph Fielding Smith:

> [Christ's] greatest suffering was in Gethsemane. We speak of the passion of Jesus Christ. A great many people have an idea that when he was on the cross, and nails were driven into his hands and feet, that was his great suffering. His great suffering was before he ever was placed upon the cross. It was in the Garden of Gethsemane that the blood oozed from the pores of his body: "Which suffering caused myself, even God, the greatest of all, to tremble because of pain, and to bleed at every pore, and to suffer both body and spirit—and would that I might not drink the bitter cup, and shrink."
>
> That was not when he was on the cross; that was in the garden. That is where he bled from every pore in his body.
>
> Now I cannot comprehend that pain.[8]

And so it was by divine decree and ordination that all things were poised for the greatest of events, the greatest of suffering, which we often refer to simply as Gethsemane. All things pointed to it. God the Father's great plan of happiness was created around it. It was the Father's will that such a thing take place. Jesus was the perfectly innocent but willing volunteer. He did not personally deserve the suffering; but it was the Father's will that he absorb it. And thereby hangs the tale, for the Savior took upon himself the full force of the punishment deserved by each member of the human family. The full force of justice was not diminished one iota for Jesus Christ. Thus, though "Jesus always deserved . . . the Father's full approval . . . when He took our sins upon Him, of divine necessity required by justice He experienced instead 'the fierceness of the wrath of Almighty God' (D&C 76:107; 88:106)."[9] That was the bitter cup. As Elder Boyd K. Packer put it, Jesus, "by choice, accepted the penalty for all mankind for the sum total of all wickedness and depravity . . . In choosing, He faced the awesome power of the evil one who was not confined to flesh nor subject to mortal pain. That was Gethsemane!"[10]

To every disciple of every dispensation, Gethsemane was and is the sweetest of victories: "From the terrible conflict in Gethsemane, Christ emerged a victor."[11] That victory means everything to us as mortals. Because of it, every human being who seeks God's love receives not only that love but also hope. Yet, to the Sinless One himself, a being of infinite goodness and perfect sensitivity, Gethsemane was the ultimate torture, the darkest hour, the starkest terror. His most extreme distress had little to do with the thought of physical death, even the hideous kind of death brought on by crucifixion. Rather, to the one Being in the universe who was personally and completely undeserving of the horrible, infinite punishments inflicted, Gethsemane was the bitterest anguish, the greatest contradiction, the gravest injustice, the bitterest of cups to drink. Yet, the will of the Father was that the bitter cup be swallowed—drained to its dregs. And drained it was, swallowed to the last drop by Christ. Thus it would be said, in ultimate irony, that the will of the Son was "swallowed up in the will of the Father" (Mosiah 15:7).

Irony and contradiction are two of the best descriptors of Gethsemane's bitter cup, which cause thoughtful disciples to reflect on the nature of tests and trials in mortality and how the lessons of the bitter cup can have profound meaning in their lives. The Prophet Joseph Smith taught that the Savior "descended in suffering below that which man can suffer; or, in other words, suffered greater sufferings, and was exposed to more powerful contradictions than any man can be."[12] Perhaps the greatest trials are those that seem the most unfair, but the faithful may take comfort in knowing that there is One who understands with perfect empathy. In Gethsemane, the contradictions that constitute the bitter cup are seen with crystal clarity. He who was the Son of the Highest descended below all things. He who was sinless was weighed down by the crushing sins of everyone else. He who was the light and the life of the world was surrounded by darkness and death. He who was sent to earth out of love, and who was characterized as Love, suffered the effects of unmitigated hatred or enmity toward God. He who was the essence of loyalty was the object of betrayal and disloyalty. He who did nothing but good suffered the greatest evil. He who was *the* Righteous One was buffeted by *the* enemy of all righteousness. But from it all, he emerged victorious.

CONCLUSION

With the coming of Jesus Christ to the New World, more than twenty-five hundred souls experienced three days that changed their lives forever, and world history was affected. For three days, God himself taught doctrines and principles that others had received in the Old World, as recorded in the New Testament. But he also said and did things of which the four Gospels have no record, and for which 3 Nephi is our treasured source. For this Fifth Gospel we should be forever grateful and perhaps much more active in filling the earth with its contents.

NOTES

1. Joseph Fielding McConkie, Robert L. Millet, Brent L. Top, *Doctrinal Commentary on the Book of Mormon*, 4 vols. (Salt Lake City: Bookcraft, 1992), 4:6.

2. "The Father and the Son: A Doctrinal Exposition by The First Presidency and the Twelve," June 30, 1916. Quoted in James E. Talmage, *Articles of Faith*. 48th ed. (Salt Lake City: The Church of Jesus Christ of Latter-day Saints, 1967), 465–473.

3. Joseph Fielding Smith, *Doctrines of Salvation*, 3 vols. (Salt Lake City: Bookcraft, 1954), 1:29–30.

4. Bruce R. McConkie, *Mormon Doctrine*, 2nd ed. (Salt Lake City: Bookcraft, 1966), 516.

5. James E. Talmage, *Jesus the Christ* (Salt Lake City: Deseret Book, 1962), 613.

6. McConkie, et. al., *Doctrinal Commentary on the Book of Mormon*, IV:41.

7. Talmage, *Jesus the Christ*, 668–69.

8. Smith, *Doctrines of Salvation*, 1:130.

9. Neal A. Maxwell, *Lord, Increase Our Faith* (Salt Lake City: Bookcraft, 1994), 13.

10. Boyd K. Packer, "Atonement, Agency, Accountability," *Ensign*, May 1988, 69.

11. Talmage, *Jesus the Christ*, 614.

12. Joseph Smith, *Lectures on Faith* (Salt Lake City: Deseret Book, 1985), 59.

2

Resurrection and Judgment

LIKE THE NEW TESTAMENT GOSPELS, 3 NEPHI FORCEFULLY TEACHES the doctrines of resurrection and judgment. In truth, the whole Book of Mormon is a prophetic testimony and explanation of the doctrine of resurrection. Third Nephi, however, contains the actual evidence and confirmation of the reality of resurrection, specifically a description of the resurrected Jesus Christ, who was the "firstfruits of them that slept," the first individual ever to be resurrected (1 Corinthians 15:20; compare 2 Nephi 2:8). The New Testament Gospels each contain accounts of Jesus as a resurrected being (Matthew 28:1–8; Mark 16:1–14; Luke 24:1–48; John 20:1–29). Likewise, 3 Nephi also presents such an account, but it is one that is richer, more detailed, and much more powerful. In fact, it might be said that while the New Testament Gospels provide a glimpse of the events associated with the Savior's Resurrection and subsequent forty-day ministry, 3 Nephi focuses brilliant illumination on the activity of his post-Resurrection ministry in the New World, thus suggesting in part what Jesus may have undertaken in the Old World after his Resurrection.

RESURRECTION

When Jesus appeared to his disciples in the Old World after three days in the tomb, he helped them to understand the nature of resurrection—that he had again taken up his physical body, the same one that had succumbed on the Cross. But he made sure they knew that he was now an immortal being of flesh and bones, never to die again. He encouraged them to discover this truth for themselves: "Behold my hands and my feet, that it is I myself: handle me, and see; for a spirit hath not flesh and bones, as ye see me have" (Luke 24:39). In his sequel to his Gospel record, Luke indicates that for forty days Jesus used the wounds of his crucifixion as teaching tools to prove that he was a resurrected being (Acts 1:1–3).

These demonstrations must have greatly impressed the Savior's followers gathered in Judea and Galilee on those occasions. But they pale in comparison to a parallel event occurring on the American continent. On that occasion, a multitude numbering some twenty-five hundred persons, including men, women, and children (see 3 Nephi 17:25), received for themselves, in a personal way, the tokens or proofs of the Lord's Resurrection:

> And it came to pass that the Lord spake unto them saying:
> Arise and come forth unto me, that ye may thrust your hands into my side, and also that ye may feel the prints of the nails in my hands and in my feet, that ye may know that I am the God of Israel, and the God of the whole earth, and have been slain for the sins of the world.
> And it came to pass that the multitude went forth, and thrust their hands into his side, and did feel the prints of the nails in his hands and in his feet; and this they did do, going forth one by one until they had all gone forth, and did see with their eyes and did feel with their hands, and did know of a surety and did bear record, that it was he, of whom it was written by the prophets, that should come.
> And when they had all gone forth and had witnessed for themselves, they did cry out with one accord, saying:
> Hosanna! Blessed be the name of the Most High God! And they did fall down at the feet of Jesus, and did worship him. (3 Nephi 11:13–17)

Among the Gospel accounts, 3 Nephi is the premier witness of Jesus's Resurrection and his post-Resurrection ministry. This alone sets it upon a high pedestal, since the Resurrection is the lynchpin of faith for all Christians. As President Howard W. Hunter taught, "The doctrine of the Resurrection is the single most fundamental and crucial doctrine in the Christian religion. It cannot be over-emphasized, nor can it be disregarded. Without the Resurrection, the gospel of Jesus Christ becomes

a litany of wise sayings and seemingly unexplainable miracles . . . with
no ultimate triumph. No, the ultimate triumph is the ultimate miracle. . . . [Jesus's] triumph over physical and spiritual death is the good
news every Christian tongue should speak."[1] Thus, if the Resurrection
is the lynchpin of the Christian faith, 3 Nephi ought to be received as a
lynchpin of textual testimonies of the resurrected Lord. It preserves for
us the testimony of the Savior himself—a living witness—that he is the
resurrected God of this world (3 Nephi 11:12–14).

"Resurrection" means to rise again or rise with power. It comes from
the Latin *resurgere* and is related to words such as *surge, resurge,* and
resurgence. It is a word immediately connoting power. Third Nephi reaf-
firms the power of the Resurrection as it confirms the testimony of other
prophets. Jacob, for one, testified of the certainty of the resurrection of *all*
human beings and even declared that resurrection itself was redemption!
It rescues all of us (except sons of perdition) from the clutches of Satan.
No greater power exists than this. Jacob exclaimed,

> O the wisdom of God, his mercy and grace! For behold, if the
> flesh should rise no more our spirits must become subject to that
> angel who fell from before the presence of the Eternal God, and
> became the devil, to rise no more.
>
> And our spirits must have become like unto him, and we become
> devils, angels to a devil, to be shut out from the presence of our God,
> and to remain with the father of lies, in misery, like unto himself;
> yea, to that being who beguiled our first parents, who transformeth
> himself nigh unto an angel of light, and stirreth up the children of
> men unto secret combinations of murder and all manner of secret
> works of darkness.
>
> O how great the goodness of our God, who prepareth a way for
> our *escape* from the grasp of this awful monster; yea, that monster,
> death and hell, which I call the death of the body, and also the death
> of the spirit.
>
> And because of the way of *deliverance* of our God, the Holy One
> of Israel, this death, of which I have spoken, which is the temporal,
> shall deliver up its dead; which death is the grave. (2 Nephi 9:8–11;
> emphasis added)

Later on, Amulek made clear that even the wicked will be resurrected:

> Therefore the wicked remain as though there had been no redemp-
> tion made, except it be the loosing of the bands of death; for behold,

the day cometh that all shall rise from the dead and stand before God, and be judged according to their works.

Now, there is a death which is called a temporal death; and the death of Christ shall loose the bands of this temporal death, that all shall be raised from this temporal death.

The spirit and the body shall be reunited again in its perfect form; both limb and joint shall be restored to its proper frame, even as we now are at this time; and we shall be brought to stand before God, knowing even as we know now, and have a bright recollection of all our guilt.

Now, this restoration shall come to all, both old and young, both bond and free, both male and female, both the wicked and the righteous; and even there shall not so much as a hair of their heads be lost; but every thing shall be restored to its perfect frame, as it is now, or in the body, and shall be brought and be arraigned before the bar of Christ the Son, and God the Father, and the Holy Spirit, which is one Eternal God, to be judged according to their works, whether they be good or whether they be evil. (Alma 11:41–44)

But the capstone testimony of the power of the Resurrection was the Lord Jesus Christ himself, which is recorded in 3 Nephi. He came among the Nephites as a risen Being and confirmed the universality of the Resurrection. During the second day of his three-day visit, he turned his attention briefly to events associated with the Second Coming but clearly had the doctrines of resurrection and judgment on his mind. The record states:

And he did expound all things, even from the beginning until the time that he should come in his glory—yea, even all things which should come upon the face of the earth, even until the elements should melt with fervent heat, and the earth should be wrapt together as a scroll, and the heavens and the earth should pass away;

And even unto the great and last day, when all people, and all kindreds, and all nations and tongues shall stand before God, to be judged of their works, whether they be good or whether they be evil—

If they be good, to the resurrection of everlasting life; and if they be evil, to the resurrection of damnation; being on a parallel, the one on the one hand and the other on the other hand, according to the mercy, and the justice, and the holiness which is in Christ, who was before the world began. (3 Nephi 26:3–5)

By the power vested in God the Father and passed on to his Son, Jesus of Nazareth rose from the dead and made it possible for each soul on earth to rise again. When Jesus's spirit reentered his physical body in the Garden Tomb that first Easter morning, he became the first person on earth to receive the keys of resurrection. It is true that he inherited *the power* to take up his body again from his Father (Elohim) at the time of his mortal birth. But he received *the keys* of resurrection only after his own resurrection. President Joseph Fielding Smith explained the sequence in this way: "Jesus Christ did for us something that we could not do for ourselves, through his infinite atonement. On the third day after the crucifixion he took up his body and gained the *keys of the Resurrection*, and thus has *power to open the graves for all men*, but this he could not do until he had first passed through death himself and conquered." [2]

This is important doctrine, for it means that the keys of resurrection are conferred *after* one has been resurrected, and those keys are then used to resurrect others. Jesus was the prototype. Having obtained the keys of resurrection himself (after his own experience with resurrection), he then had the power to resurrect all others. According to President Brigham Young, those keys of resurrection first acquired by the Savior are then further given, extended, or delegated to others who have died and been resurrected. "They will be ordained, by those who hold the keys of the resurrection, to go forth and resurrect the Saints, just as we receive the ordinances of baptism, then the keys of authority to baptize others." [3]

Before Jesus was resurrected, only his Father, our Father in Heaven, possessed the keys of resurrection (even though as the Son of God, he possessed the power of life in himself—independently). After he was resurrected, Jesus acquired the keys of resurrection, which could then be given to others. As a result of his own resurrection, Jesus now controls all power and all keys, under the direction of his Father, which he delegates to others as they are worthy and become prepared to possess the various powers of godliness. These powers are then used to bless the human family. This is true for the keys of resurrection and all other power and authority.

Immediately after Jesus's Resurrection, many righteous souls—ancient saints—came forth from their graves. Matthew records: "And the graves were opened; and many bodies of the saints which slept arose. And came out of the graves after his resurrection, and went into the holy city, and appeared unto many" (Matthew 27:52–53). On the American continent (even before the birth of Jesus), it was understood that following the Resurrection of Jesus, the righteous dead would participate in the first resurrection—those having lived from Adam to Jesus Christ. The prophet Abinadi taught:

> For were it not for the redemption which he hath made for his people, which was prepared from the foundation of the world, I say unto you, were it not for this, all mankind must have perished.
>
> But behold, the bands of death shall be broken, and the Son reigneth, and hath power over the dead; therefore, he bringeth to pass the resurrection of the dead.
>
> And there cometh a resurrection, even a first resurrection; yea, even a resurrection of those that have been, and who are, and who shall be, even until the resurrection of Christ—for so shall he be called.
>
> And now, the resurrection of all the prophets, and all those that have believed in their words, or all those that have kept the commandments of God, shall come forth in the first resurrection; therefore, they are the first resurrection.
>
> They are raised to dwell with God who has redeemed them; thus they have eternal life through Christ, who has broken the bands of death.
>
> And these are those who have part in the first resurrection; and these are they that have died before Christ came, in their ignorance, not having salvation declared unto them. And thus the Lord bringeth about the restoration of these; and they have a part in the first resurrection, or have eternal life, being redeemed by the Lord. (Mosiah 15:19–24)

Five years before the birth of Jesus Christ, the prophet Samuel spoke of the Messiah's Resurrection and those who would follow, in language akin to the Gospel of Matthew: "And many graves shall be opened, and shall yield up many of their dead; and many saints shall appear unto many" (Helaman 14:25). When our resurrected Lord appeared to those on the American continent he referred to Samuel's prophecy:

> And it came to pass that he said unto Nephi: Bring forth the record which ye have kept.
>
> And when Nephi had brought forth the records, and laid them before him, he cast his eyes upon them and said:
>
> Verily I say unto you, I commanded my servant Samuel, the Lamanite, that he should testify unto this people, that at the day that the Father should glorify his name in me that there were many

saints who should arise from the dead, and should appear unto many, and should minister unto them. And he said unto them: Was it not so?

And his disciples answered him and said: Yea, Lord, Samuel did prophesy according to thy words, and they were all fulfilled.

And Jesus said unto them: How be it that ye have not written this thing, that many saints did arise and appear unto many and did minister unto them?

And it came to pass that Nephi remembered that this thing had not been written.

And it came to pass that Jesus commanded that it should be written; therefore it was written according as he commanded. (3 Nephi 23:7–13)

This passage in the Fifth Gospel is significant and instructive. We see that Jesus himself was the very editor of the record. No other Gospel can make that claim! This no doubt is one of the reasons the Prophet Joseph Smith could proclaim the Book of Mormon to be the most correct of any book on earth (it is humbling to realize that we possess it). And the thing Jesus wanted to have crystal clear in his record—for 3 Nephi is *his* record—was the doctrine of resurrection.

MANY JUDGMENTS

Instructively, the Book of Mormon often mentions resurrection and judgment together. They seem to be regarded as companion doctrines. One reason for this is the fact that at the time of the resurrection, every individual who has ever lived on earth will be brought back into the presence of God and "be judged according to their works" (3 Nephi 27:15; see also Alma 11:40–43). The words of Samuel the Lamanite are clear that all will be brought back into God's presence, even if only for a time:

For behold, he surely must die that salvation may come; yea, it behooveth him and becometh expedient that he dieth, to bring to pass the resurrection of the dead, that thereby men may be brought into the presence of the Lord.

Yea, behold, this death bringeth to pass the resurrection, and redeemeth all mankind from the first death—that spiritual death; for all mankind, by the fall of Adam being cut off from the presence of the Lord, are considered as dead, both as to things temporal and to things spiritual.

But behold, the resurrection of Christ redeemeth mankind, yea, even all mankind, and bringeth them back into the presence of the Lord.

Yea, and it bringeth to pass the condition of repentance, that whosoever repenteth the same is not hewn down and cast into the fire; but whosoever repenteth not is hewn down and cast into the fire; and there cometh upon them again a spiritual death, yea, a second death, for they are cut off again as to things pertaining to righteousness. (Helaman 14:15–18)

While it is true that there will be a final judgment, when every soul who has ever lived will stand before God and receive God's official pronouncement, it is also true that there will be intermediate judgments before the final judgment and that these intermediate judgments will affect the resurrection of the dead—both in terms of timing and of condition. At the time of death, we will be judged as to our fitness for either paradise or spirit prison (see Alma 40:11–14). And before the resurrection takes place, we will be judged again as to our worthiness to receive either a celestial, terrestrial, or telestial body. The righteous, those in paradise, will be resurrected first (Mosiah 15:21–25; Alma 40:16–20; D&C 88:95–98; D&C 76:50–70; D&C 133:54–55). The kind of physical body we receive when we are resurrected will be the body we will possess in eternity, and that body will determine our potential and eternal possibilities (1 Corinthians 15:40–42; D&C 76; D&C 88:14–24). For example, those possessing celestial bodies will enjoy life with God and will possess the ability to become like our Heavenly Parents if married for eternity by Priesthood authority. Those who receive terrestrial bodies in the resurrection are limited in terms of place and potential. They cannot go where God and Christ dwell in "worlds without end" (D&C 76:112). They cannot have eternal increase (D&C 130:4). Every individual "shall be judged according to their works, and every man shall receive according to his own works, his own dominion, in the mansions which are prepared" (D&C 76:111). Much of this judging occurs *before* the resurrection.

HIERARCHY OF JUDGES

God is a perfect Being and therefore the perfect Judge. Jesus acknowledged that while all judgment ultimately rests with God the Father, the latter delegated judgment to the Son: "For the Father judgeth no man, but hath committed all judgment unto the Son: That all men should honour the Son, even as they honour the Father" (John 5:22–23). Furthermore, in other passages in the New Testament Gospels, Jesus taught that not only has the Son been delegated responsibility for judgment but also that he has, in turn, delegated that task to the Twelve: "And Jesus said unto them, Verily I say unto you, That ye which have followed me, in the regeneration when the Son of man shall sit in the throne of his glory, ye also shall sit upon twelve thrones, judging the twelve tribes of Israel" (Matthew 19:28; see Luke 22:30). In 3 Nephi, Jesus verifies his Father's role in all judgment, and then delegates judgment to the Nephite Twelve for their own people: "And behold, all things are written by the Father; therefore out of the books which shall be written shall the world be judged. And know ye that ye shall be judges of this people, according to the judgment which I shall give unto you" (3 Nephi 27:27).

This doctrine of the delegation of judgment was summarized specifically for the people of the latter days by the prophet Mormon more than three hundred years after Christ's visit to the New World. He said,

> Yea, behold, I write unto all the ends of the earth; yea, unto you, twelve tribes of Israel, who shall be judged according to your works by the twelve whom Jesus chose to be his disciples in the land of Jerusalem.
>
> And I write also unto the remnant of this people, who shall also be judged by the twelve whom Jesus chose in this land; and they shall be judged by the other twelve whom Jesus chose in the land of Jerusalem.
>
> And these things doth the Spirit manifest unto me; therefore I write unto you all. And for this cause I write unto you, that ye may know that ye must all stand before the judgment-seat of Christ, yea, every soul who belongs to the whole human family of Adam; and ye must stand to be judged of your works, whether they be good or evil. (Mormon 3:18–20)

Indeed, it seems there will be a whole hierarchy of judges who will act under Jesus Christ to judge all the posterity of Adam and Eve. Elder Bruce R. McConkie wrote:

> Under Christ, selected agents and representatives shall sit in judgment upon specified peoples and nations. Scriptural intimations indicate that there will be a great judicial hierarchy, each judge acting in his own sphere of appointment and in conformity with

the eternal principles of judgment which are in Christ. When John wrote of that day of judgment incident to the Second Coming of our Lord, he said: 'I saw thrones, and they sat upon them, and judgment was given unto them' (Rev. 20:4)."[4]

However, we may rest assured that all judgments will be in harmony with the will of the Father and the Son, and final decrees of damnation for the wicked will be issued by Deity alone.[5]

It should not be hard for Latter-day Saints to appreciate the concept of a hierarchy of judges. First of all, the Book of Mormon teaches that each of us will judge ourselves. Some of the greatest punishment that can come to individuals in this life, and certainly a principle source of punishment after mortality, derives from remorse of conscience. Young Alma hints at this when he describes his wicked state and subsequent reclamation! "I was in the darkest abyss . . . my soul was racked with eternal torment; but I am snatched, and my soul is pained no more" (Mosiah 27:29).

Jacob understood that the great judgment in the spirit world comes when a man sees himself as he is seen. Furthermore, in the resurrection, "all men become incorruptible, and immortal, and they are living souls, having a perfect knowledge like unto us in the flesh, save it be that our knowledge shall be perfect. Wherefore, we shall have a perfect knowledge of all our guilt, and our uncleanness and our nakedness; and the righteous shall have a perfect knowledge of their enjoyment, and their righteousness, being clothed with purity, yea, even with the robe of righteousness" (2 Nephi 9:13–14).

Others, including Alma and Moroni, point out that the state of mind shall bring happiness or misery to individuals (Alma 40:11–14). The latter asks, "Do ye suppose that ye shall dwell with him under a consciousness of guilt? Do ye suppose that ye could be happy to dwell with that holy Being, when your souls are racked with a consciousness of guilt that ye have ever abused his laws? Behold, I say unto you that ye would be more miserable to dwell with a holy and just God, under a consciousness of your filthiness before him, than ye would to dwell with the damned souls in hell. For behold, when ye shall be brought to see your nakedness before God, and also the glory of God, and the holiness of Jesus Christ, it will kindle a flame of unquenchable fire upon you" (Mormon 9:3–5).

After self-judgment comes the judgment of authorized priesthood leaders, who also pass judgment upon us as we live our lives in mortality. Each of us is required to submit ourselves to the authority of the bishop (or branch president), whose assigned task is to act as a judge in Israel and determine individual worthiness. The bishop serves under the jurisdiction of the stake president, who serves under the direction of area authorities, or area presidency, who serve at the discretion of the Quorum of the Twelve, and so forth until all men and women come under the all-seeing eye of the Lord.

The Lord and his prophets are not bothered by seemingly mathematical puzzles and neither should we be; for, as it is in the Church of God on earth, where ordinances and covenants are administered by many servants, so it is in the realm of eternal judgments. They are administered by those commissioned of God.

Since none will be able to ignore or escape judgment ultimately presided over by Jesus Christ, all humankind will be drawn to the Savior just as he declared to his disciples in the New World (3 Nephi 27:14–15). Being drawn to him is thus inescapable, and thankfully so, for he is the Perfect Judge.

CRITERIA FOR JUDGMENT

As we know from many passages in the Bible and the Book of Mormon, judgment will be based on an individual's works and actions in mortality. But Alma hints at something more: "For our words will condemn us, yea, all our works will condemn us; we shall not be found spotless; and our thoughts will also condemn us; and in this awful state we shall not dare to look up to our God; and we would fain be glad if we could command the rocks and the mountains to fall upon us to hide us from his presence" (Alma 12:14).

From the revelations given to many prophets, both ancient and modern, we gain a more complete understanding of the criteria employed by the Lord to ensure a perfectly just and a perfectly merciful judgment for each of our Heavenly Father's children.

1. Individuals will be judged not only according to their works, but also according to the desires and intents of their hearts (D&C 137:9; 33:1; Alma 41:3).
2. Individuals will be judged according to the degree of knowledge they possess and the opportunities available to them during their mortal probation (2 Nephi 9:25–27; Moroni 8:22; Mosiah 15:24–26).
3. Individuals will be judged according to records kept both on earth

and in heaven (2 Nephi 29:11; D&C 128:6–7; Revelation 20:12).

4. Individuals will know that their rewards or punishments are just (2 Nephi 9:46; Mosiah 27:31) and that their judgments constitute a proper and appropriate decision (Mosiah 16:1; 29:12).

Without question, when Jesus speaks of his right and responsibility to issue judgment, as he does in the New Testament Gospels and in 3 Nephi, we may know with a surety that those judgments are made in accord with perfect justice and perfect mercy. In the end, I believe the assertion of President J. Reuben Clark will come true. He said, "I believe when the Lord metes out punishment, he will mete out the least possible punishment that it is possible to mete out and satisfy the demands of justice; and when he metes out rewards for the good things we have done, for keeping the commandments, he will mete out the greatest possible number of blessings for that which we have done that is right."[6]

Regarding God's capability to judge fairly, the scriptures teach that "Righteousness and judgment are the habitation of his throne" (Psalm 97:2). "He is the Rock, his work is perfect: for all his ways are judgment: a God of truth and without iniquity, just and righteous is he" (Deuteronomy 32:4). "Judgment goeth before the face of him who sitteth upon the throne and governeth and executeth all things" (D&C 88:40).

MAKING PERSONAL JUDGMENTS

In the New Testament, it is recorded that Jesus Christ commanded his disciples not to judge, lest they themselves be judged with that same kind and measure of judgment. "Judge not, that ye be not judged. For with what judgment ye judge, ye shall be judged: and with what measure ye mete, it shall be measured to you again" (Matthew 7:1–2). Jesus used the same words to his New World disciples (3 Nephi 14:1–2). Yet, just a few verses later, in both Matthew and in 3 Nephi, the Savior commanded his disciples to do things which could not be fulfilled unless they *did* make judgments and evaluations of others. He said, for example, "Beware of false prophets. . . . Ye shall know them by their fruits" (Matthew 7:15–16; 3 Nephi 14:15–16). Again, the language is the same in both accounts.

The apparent contradiction is resolved for us in the Joseph Smith Translation, a doctrinal clarification the Prophet was inspired to record. "Now these are the words which Jesus taught his disciples that they should say unto the people. Judge not unrighteously, that ye be not judged: but judge righteous judgment" (JST, Matthew 7:1–2). It becomes obvious that Jesus's intention was to warn disciples against unrighteous judgment, against hypocritical or self-righteous judgment, against making judgments without knowledge of attendant circumstances, against embracing uninspired judgments, or against acting beyond the bounds of one's stewardship. Jesus implied similar ideas in Matthew 23:13–39. And the Apostle Paul also said something similar in Romans 2:1. The latter said: "You, therefore, have no excuse, you who pass judgment on someone else, for at whatever point you judge the other, you are condemning yourself, because you who pass judgment do the same things" (Romans 2:1, New International Version). Why Jesus did not simply clarify what he meant in the Gospel accounts (Matthew and 3 Nephi) may be as simple as the idea that neither group of disciples anciently needed clarification. They understood his intended purpose and meaning. Disciples today, far removed from the early disciples in chronology and culture, benefit from the clarification supplied by Joseph Smith.

CONCLUSION

In truth, faithful disciples of Jesus Christ in this last dispensation will need, as never before, increased powers of righteous judgment and discernment. As in early Christian times, the adversary uses every tool to deceive the Lord's followers—even to the point of appearing as an angel of light (compare 2 Corinthians 11:14 and D&C 128:20, 129:8). Both the New Testament Gospels and 3 Nephi preserve the powerful warnings and exhortations of Jesus Christ, as well as a correct understanding of the doctrines of resurrection and judgment. And thus we see the wisdom of those who have referred to 3 Nephi as the Fifth Gospel and have lived their lives by its counsel.

Understanding correctly the doctrines of resurrection and judgment as taught by Jesus Christ in 3 Nephi and by his authorized servants elsewhere in the Book of Mormon can greatly help individuals discern truth from error. Misunderstanding these doctrines can lead to deception and ultimately to poor choices and destructive behavior. This was precisely the problem with one prophet's son—Corianton. Because he did not understand the doctrine of resurrection and judgment, nor their power in shaping and determining a person's possibilities and potential in the eternities, he engaged in serious misdeeds. His father, Alma, spent a great deal of time counseling him and trying to reclaim him. This effort gave to us some of the most powerful chapters on resurrection and judgment in the Book of Mormon—Alma 39–42.

Alma understood the root of the problem, which was lack of doctrinal understanding regarding resurrection and judgment. This becomes clear from statements he made as he counseled with his son:

> Now my son, here is somewhat more I would say unto thee; for I perceive that thy mind is worried concerning the resurrection of the dead . . .
>
> And now, my son, I have somewhat to say concerning the restoration of which has been spoken; for behold, some have wrested the scriptures, and have gone far astray because of this thing. And I perceive that thy mind has been worried also concerning this thing. But behold, I will explain it unto thee . . .
>
> And now, my son, I perceive there is somewhat more which doth worry your mind, which ye cannot understand—which is concerning the justice of God in the punishment of the sinner; for ye do try to suppose that it is injustice that the sinner should be consigned to a state of misery. (Alma 40:1; 41:1; 42:1)

Alma's perceptive evaluation of his son's predicament might serve as an example to parents who have children with behavioral challenges. Is it possible that sometimes lack of doctrinal understanding could be a significant source of the problem? A correct knowledge of the Resurrection and Judgment makes a difference. It did for Corianton. And obviously the Savior felt it would for twenty-five hundred souls gathered at the temple in the land Bountiful. It can change lives and behavior. As President Boyd K. Packer rightly stated, "True doctrine, understood, changes attitudes and behavior. The study of the doctrines of the gospel will improve behavior quicker than a study of behavior will improve behavior. Preoccupation with unworthy behavior can lead to unworthy behavior. That is why we stress so forcefully the study of the doctrines of the gospel." [7]

Elder Neal A. Maxwell also helped us to see why a sound understanding of the doctrines of the gospel will aid our quest for perfection. He said, "Doctrines believed and practiced do change and improve us, while ensuring our vital access to the Spirit. Both outcomes are crucial." [8]

NOTES

1. Howard W. Hunter, Conference Report, April 1986, 18.

2. Joseph Fielding Smith, *Doctrines of Salvation* (Salt Lake City: Bookcraft, 1954), 1:128.

3. John A. Widtsoe, *Discourses of Brigham Young* (Salt Lake City: Deseret Book, 1966), 398.

4. Bruce R. McConkie, *Mormon Doctrine* (Salt Lake City: Bookcraft, 1966), 398.

5. Bruce R. McConkie, *The Millennial Messiah*, (Salt Lake City: Deseret Book, 1982), 520.

6. J. Reuben Clark Jr., "As We Sow, So Shall We Reap," Brigham Young University address, recorded May 3, 1955. Online resource.

7. Boyd K. Packer, Conference Report, October 1986, 20.

8. Neal A. Maxwell, *One More Strain of Praise* (Salt Lake City: Bookcraft, 1999), x.

3

The Temple Context of the Fifth Gospel

AN ARRESTING FEATURE OF THE FIFTH GOSPEL IS ITS CONNECTION TO the temple. Jesus's "appearance at the temple invites the idea that his words have something important to do with teachings and ordinances found within the temple."[1] Third Nephi is a temple-centered text. In this regard, it is like the New Testament Gospels.

TEMPLE IN THE NEW TESTAMENT

Beginning with the four Gospels and ending with the book of Revelation, the temple is front and center in the New Testament. The temple was important to the New Testament writers. "In spite of the different approaches taken by each of the four Evangelists, one strong thread that runs through the earliest memories about Christ in all four Gospels is the centrality of the temple for Jesus."[2] The story of Jesus's life and ministry begins in the temple with the vision given to Zacharias, John the Baptist's father (Luke 1:5–22). When only forty days old, Jesus made his first appearance at the temple (Luke 2:22–38). He was found in the temple at age twelve (Luke 2:41–47), and during his mortal life, he cleansed the temple twice (John 2:14; Matthew 21:13). The four New Testament Gospels powerfully affirm that Jesus taught daily in the temple (Matthew 21:23; 26:55; Mark 11:27; 12:35–40; 14:49; Luke 19:45–48;

20:1; 21:37; 22:52; John 7:28; 10:23). The great symbol of the end of the Mosaic dispensation, the end of the Aaronic order of the temple, the end of divinely sanctioned animal sacrifices, and the beginning of a new era, was the tearing of the veil of the temple into two pieces when Jesus died (Matthew 27:51; Mark 15:38; and Luke 23:45). After his resurrection, Jesus commanded his Apostles to stay in Jerusalem, at the temple, until they were endowed with power from on high—which they did (Luke 24:49, 53).

The Apostle John's writings, intended for members of the Church of Jesus Christ, perhaps even endowed members, are filled with allusions to temple teachings and ordinances. One example is John's unique report of Jesus instituting the ordinance of the washing of the feet during the Last Supper (see John 13:4–10). Elder Bruce R. McConkie of the Quorum of the Twelve called this "a holy and sacred rite, one performed by the saints in the seclusion of their temple sanctuaries."[3] Other examples abound. The first three chapters of the book of Revelation are filled with allusions to, and images found in, the temple. Representative statements include, "To him that overcometh will I [God] give . . . a white stone, and in the stone a new name" (Revelation 2:17); "He that overcometh, the same shall be clothed in white raiment" (3:5); "Him that overcometh will I make a pillar in the temple of my God" (3:12); "To him that overcometh will I grant to sit with me in my throne, even as I also overcame, and am set down with my Father in his throne" (3:21).

The book of Revelation ends with John's startling announcement that in the celestial city of Jerusalem he "saw no temple therein" (Revelation 21:22). This is noteworthy because the temple had always played a major role, in one way or another, in Jerusalem's and Israel's history. But in the celestial world, says John, "the Lord God Almighty and the Lamb are the temple of [celestial Jerusalem]" (Revelation 21:22).

NEW WORLD TEMPLE CONTEXT

It is obvious that the temple was of towering importance to Jesus and his disciples in the Old World. Therefore, it seems not only natural but perhaps expected that Third Nephi be centered around the temple. What more natural place in the New World could there have been for Jesus to come and teach than the temple—the place where he was accustomed to teach during his mortal life. Thus, his appearance at the temple in the land Bountiful (3 Nephi 11:1) was no random or accidental occurrence. Of all the places Jesus could have chosen to make his New World appearance—palace, market, city gate, or wooded grove—Jesus came to the temple and firmly fixed the importance of the temple setting for what transpired over the next three days. During our resurrected Lord's forty-day ministry in the Old World, temple-centered teachings were at the heart of his activity, as some enlightened ancient writers indicated. First, we have the witness of Luke, whose sequel to his Gospel account, the Acts of the Apostles or book of Acts, begins by indicating what the forty-day ministry was all about. He says, "The former treatise have I made, O Theophilus, of all that Jesus began both to do and teach, Until the day in which he was taken up, after that he through the Holy Ghost had given commandments unto the apostles whom he had chosen: To whom also he shewed himself alive after his passion by many infallible proofs, being seen of them forty days, and speaking of the things pertaining to the kingdom of God" (Acts 1:1–3).

In other words, after his suffering ("passion" in the King James Version) and Resurrection, Jesus came to the Apostles for forty days, showed himself to be alive by many "infallible proofs," and taught them those matters (doctrine, ordinances, organization) associated with the kingdom of God. The Greek word which the King James Bible translates as "infallible proofs" is *tekmeriois*, but it literally means "sure signs and tokens." Jesus's proof of his resurrection were the tokens in his hands, feet, and side, but they were also the tools by which Jesus taught his apostles about the most important matters pertaining to the kingdom of God. These tokens were and are also at the heart of temple worship, both ancient and modern. The signs and tokens of the Savior's atoning sacrifice are part of the endowment ordinance. The Prophet Joseph Smith taught on several occasions that the gospel of Jesus Christ has required the same ordinances and powers to save souls in every dispensation.

> Ordinances instituted *in the heavens before the foundation of the world*, in the priesthood, for the salvation of men, are not to be altered or changed. *All must be saved on the same principles.* . . .
> One of the ordinances of the house of the Lord is baptism for the dead. *God decreed before the foundation of the world* that that ordinance should be administered in a font prepared for that purpose in the house of the Lord . . .
> If a man gets a fullness of the priesthood of God he has to get it in

the same way that Jesus Christ obtained it, and that was by *keeping all the commandments* and obeying all the ordinances *of the house of the Lord* . . .

All men who become heirs of God and joint heirs with Jesus Christ *will have to receive the fullness of the ordinances of his kingdom*; and those who will not receive all the ordinances will come short of the fullness of that glory, if they do not lose the whole.[4]

President Heber C. Kimball taught plainly that the temple endowment in this dispensation was found in the ancient Church. Jesus "inducted his Apostles into these ordinances."[5] That the ancient Apostles had this instruction and these ordinances is obvious from John's opening statements in his Apocalypse: "John to the seven churches which are in Asia: Grace be unto you, and peace, from him which is, and which was, and which is to come . . . And from Jesus Christ, who is the faithful witness, and the first begotten of the dead, and the prince of the kings of the earth. Unto him that loved us, and washed us from our sins in his own blood, *And hath made us kings and priests unto God and his Father*" (Revelation 1:4–6; emphasis added).

Centuries after the original Apostles were long gone, descriptions of Jesus's forty-day ministry as a temple-centered experience persisted. The preeminent fourth-century church historian, Eusebius (ca. 260–340), attributed holiness to a certain cave on the southern end of the Mount of Olives because special sacred teachings were given there by Jesus to his closest associates. Consistent with a general picture of the era that emerges in various scriptural and non-biblical texts, Eusebius says that it was Constantine's mother, St. Helena, "who on her arrival in the Holy Land ([AD] 326) had a church built over the mystical grotto of the Mount of Olives, the very place where, according to accurate history, the Saviour had stayed and had revealed the sacred mysteries to his disciples."[6]

Did Jesus also instruct and initiate his New World disciples into the mysteries—those divine, sacred secrets that only the worthy can know—when he spent three days with them, as recorded in 3 Nephi? Without a doubt. We need only reread Joseph Smith's statement above to know that it is true, but there are other indicators.

First, Nephite temples were well established as locales where the mysteries of the kingdom of God were delivered. A good example involves King Benjamin. Mosiah, by request of his father, issued a proclamation throughout the land, "that thereby they might gather themselves together, to go up to the temple to hear the words which his father should speak unto them" (Mosiah 1:18; 2:1). The people came up to the temple in families and "pitched their tents round about the temple, every man having his tent with the door thereof toward the temple, that thereby they might remain in their tents and hear the words which king Benjamin should speak unto them" (Mosiah 2:6). When King Benjamin began to speak he revealed the purpose for which he had gathered them—to teach the mysteries of holiness: "And these are the words which he spake and caused to be written, saying: My brethren, all ye that have assembled yourselves together, you that can hear my words which I shall speak unto you this day; for I have not commanded you to come up hither to trifle with the words which I shall speak, but that you should hearken unto me, and open your ears that ye may hear, and your hearts that ye may understand, and your minds that *the mysteries of God* may be unfolded to your view" (Mosiah 2:9; emphasis added; see also Alma 12:9; 13:3, 16).

Revelation of the mysteries of the kingdom of God and the Lord's temples go together. That was true in the New World before the resurrected Lord's appearance. And it was true when the Savior appeared at the temple in Bountiful after his resurrection. Evidence for this assertion includes the nature of the teachings that are preserved, including the sermon at the temple that parallels the Sermon on the Mount, as well as matters that could not be recorded. During the first day of his visit to his American Israelites, one of the first things Jesus did was deliver a discourse that has at its heart instruction concerning celestial living (see our discussion on 3 Nephi 12–14 in chapter four). Shortly afterward, the Savior asked his twenty-five hundred listeners to go to their homes to ponder, pray, and prepare for the instruction to come on the following day (3 Nephi 17:3). He then performed miracles to heal all the sick and infirm. So great was the faith of the people that he commanded the little children to be brought to him, asked all to kneel on the ground, and then prayed things that "cannot be written" (3 Nephi 17:15).

HEAVEN AND EARTH TOGETHER

Perhaps at no other time in Book of Mormon history were heaven and earth drawn so near to each other. Not only did Jesus pray unspeakable things, but the multitude also saw Jesus do things that could not be described, as the record implies:

And when he had said these words, he himself also knelt upon the earth; and behold he prayed unto the Father, and the things which he prayed cannot be written, and the multitude did bear record who heard him.

And after this manner do they bear record: The eye hath never seen, neither hath the ear heard, before, so great and marvelous things as we saw and heard Jesus speak unto the Father;

And no tongue can speak, neither can there be written by any man, neither can the hearts of men conceive so great and marvelous things as we both saw and heard Jesus speak; and no one can conceive of the joy which filled our souls at the time we heard him pray for us unto the Father.

And it came to pass that when Jesus had made an end of praying unto the Father, he arose; but so great was the joy of the multitude that they were overcome. (3 Nephi 17:15–18)

Perhaps this is why we do not have more accounts in the scriptures of Jesus praying. Things too sacred to be shared publicly were part of his prayers among those who were filled with faith. Not only that, but the people with Jesus would have been left speechless—"overcome" with joy and gratitude for the presence of the God of this world, the very Creator of heaven and earth, as they were on that occasion. In addition, Jesus himself may have been overcome—moved by great emotion, love, and compassion—as he was in this instance preserved by Mormon (3 Nephi 17:20–22). We know from the New Testament Gospels that compassion was a hallmark of Jesus's personality and formed the basis of his interactions with those whose faith allowed an environment of love and trust to prevail. We know this was true of this episode involving the little children. Before he prayed with the multitude, Jesus had told them, "my bowels are filled with compassion towards you" (3 Nephi 17:6). This compassion is evident when he wept after his prayer, took the little children one by one and blessed them, and then wept again.

Matthew's Gospel suggests that little children were always a special delight to our Lord (Matthew 18:1–6); 3 Nephi seems to confirm this belief (3 Nephi 17:15–21). In this regard, President Boyd K. Packer of the Quorum of the Twelve provided this insight: "This is the Church of Jesus Christ. It is His Church. He is our Exemplar, our Redeemer. We are commanded to be 'even as He is' (1 John 3:7). He was a teacher of children. He commanded His disciples at Jerusalem to 'suffer little children, and forbid them not, to come unto me: for of such is the kingdom of heaven' (Matthew 19:14). In the account of the Savior's ministry among the Nephites, we can see deeper into His soul perhaps than at any other place."[7]

The weeping Savior of 3 Nephi is the same Being who showed his emotions in the Old World (see John 11:35). Ours is a God of deep feeling. He himself experiences profound happiness and sadness for us; we are never far from his thoughts nor from his heart. As the author of Hebrews declared, we don't worship a high priest who cannot be touched with the feeling of our infirmities (Hebrews 4:15), but rather we reverence a God who was "made like unto his brethren, that he might be a merciful and faithful high priest . . . For in that he himself hath suffered being tempted, he is able to succor them that are tempted" (Hebrews 2:17–18).

The crowning result of Jesus's prayer and interaction with the children at the temple was an unparalleled demonstration of the very environment of heaven itself, the celestial glory, that came to earth that day. As is recorded,

> And [Jesus] spake unto the multitude, and said unto them: Behold your little ones. And as they looked to behold they cast their eyes towards heaven, and they saw angels descending out of heaven as it were in the midst of fire; and they came down and encircled those little ones about, and they were encircled about with fire; and the angels did minister unto them. And the multitude did see and hear and bear record; and they know that their record is true for they all of them did see and hear, every man for himself; and they were in number about two thousand and five hundred souls; and they did consist of men, women, and children. (3 Nephi 17:23–25)

The sacred, supernal, and glorious environment in which God the Father himself dwells was made manifest on earth at this time. The "fire" spoken of in 3 Nephi 17:24 is a way to describe God's tremendous glory. The Prophet Joseph Smith said several times that God and all the righteous dwell in "everlasting burnings in immortal glory," that the Almighty himself "dwells in eternal fire; flesh and blood cannot go there, for all corruption is devoured by the fire. 'Our God is a consuming fire' . . . [and] our flesh is quickened by the Spirit."[8] Thus, the environment of celestial glory encircled the little children. The environment *at* the temple in Bountiful became, as it were, the environment that exists *in* the temple. The area outside of the temple became a large, open-air house of the Lord. The little children became quickened or were made alive by the Spirit of God. Impurities were burned out of them. They were made pure and incorruptible at that moment, for that time. And twenty-five hundred individuals did see, hear, and feel that which transpired.

SEALING OF FAMILIES

Our understanding of what transpired at the temple in the land Bountiful can only remain incomplete until each of us is actually encircled about by eternal fire and we experience for ourselves personally the environment in which the Father and the Son dwell. For one thing, human language alone prevents us from understanding because human communication is imperfect. The Prophet Joseph Smith stated: "Reading the experience of others, or the revelation given to *them*, can never give *us* a comprehensive view of our condition and true relation to God. Knowledge of these things can only be obtained by experience through the ordinances of God set forth for that purpose. Could you gaze into heaven five minutes, you would know more than you would by reading all that ever was written on the subject." [9] We cannot conceive things that only the Spirit can teach. Neither can we know everything that transpired between the Father, the Son, angels, and mortals on that occasion. It was not recorded! However, we can read between the lines to gain a little more insight. At least five ideas occur to us:

First, in addition to the limitation of human language, another reason that most of what was seen and heard cannot be written is that some matters of the Lord are so sacred that they require a higher level of worthiness and must remain secret to the profane world—just as we note regarding Latter-day Saint temples today. The environment of temple holiness existed in rich abundance at Bountiful because of the exceptional faith displayed by the multitude.

Second, Jesus not only prayed a marvelous prayer, but also the record says he prayed *for* "us"—the adults, the parents of the children, those who kept the record (3 Nephi 17:17).

Third, upon rising, Jesus "took" the little children, and touched them one by one. It is no great leap of imagination to suppose the Savior gave his blessings and performed his ordinances by the laying on of hands at that time (3 Nephi 17:21).

Fourth, he called upon the adults—the parents forming the multitude—to "behold" their little ones, to gaze upon their family groups

(3 Nephi 17:23). It is obvious that families were of paramount importance to Jesus. By calling upon parents in that setting to behold their little ones, Jesus also provided a pattern for parents today. Elder M. Russell Ballard of the Quorum of the Twelve said that to him this means "that we should embrace them [our children] with our eyes and with our hearts; we should see and appreciate them for who they really are: spirit children of our Heavenly Father, with divine attributes. When we truly behold our little ones, we behold the glory, wonder, and majesty of God, our Eternal Father. . . . They are receptive to the truth because they have no preconceived notions; everything is real to children. . . . Their souls are endowed naturally with divine potential that is infinite and eternal." [10]

Fifth, with the coming of angels and fire from heaven, it is possible that the earthly multitude both witnessed the ratification of those actions performed by the Savior (the Holy Ghost putting his seal on them), and that they saw angelic witnesses testify of the validity of all those things that were said and were done. In a modern revelation, the Lord explained that all covenants and performances must be sealed by the Holy Ghost, who is the Holy Spirit of Promise, to have force after this life (D&C 132:7, 18–19, 26).

Much of the foregoing leads us to conclude that what transpired at the temple in the land Bountiful included the ordinance of sealing children to their parents in the presence of holy witnesses. [11] In fact, it seems to me that what we read about in 3 Nephi 17 is an account of the sealing together of generations in the great family of God. The coming of angels to the children on that occasion seems to suggest heavenly messengers with a special interest in those children (family members of previous generations) coming to acknowledge the completion, the welding together, of that portion of the family circle. Remember, the angelic messengers "came down and *encircled* those little ones about" (3 Nephi 17:24; emphasis added). The image that comes to my mind is that of a family circle and a family embrace.

It is not surprising that later on in the course of his three-day ministry, the Savior commanded the Nephite leaders to record the words of the prophet Malachi (chapters 3 and 4) so that the people would have "the words which the Father had given unto Malachi" (3 Nephi 24:1). Remember that the plates of brass predated Malachi's time frame (around 430 BC) and thus did not contain his writings or other sacred writings. And of all the things the Savior could have chosen to restore—from

Malachi or any of the other prophets and writings which the Nephites did not possess—he chose to give them Malachi 3 and 4.

Note how Malachi 3 begins, or at least how the Savior quoted it: "Thus said the Father unto Malachi—Behold, I will send my messenger, and he shall prepare the way before me, and the Lord whom ye seek shall suddenly come to his temple, even the messenger of the covenant, whom ye delight in" (3 Nephi 24:1). Furthermore, note how Malachi 4 ends, as Jesus quoted it: "Behold, I will send you Elijah the prophet before the coming of the great and dreadful day of the Lord; And he shall turn the heart of the fathers to the children, and the heart of the children to their fathers, lest I come and smite the earth with a curse" (3 Nephi 25:5–6). These temple texts speak to the importance of family connections. When Jesus commanded the Nephite remnant to behold their little ones, he was helping to fulfill Malachi's promise that "the heart of the fathers" would turn to the children. Surely we can see that during the Savior's three-day visit to the New World, much more was going on than meets the eye. Jesus's instruction was rooted in temple-oriented activity.

CONCLUSION

Other things transpired on the first day of Jesus's visit to the Nephites. He instituted the sacrament (3 Nephi 18:1–14), taught the true order and purpose of prayer (3 Nephi 18:15–21), testified that he was and is the light of the world (compare 3 Nephi 18:16 and 15:9), and he gave the Twelve witnesses a special blessing and commission (3 Nephi 18:36–38). These are all acts that were performed in the Old World and were appropriate to a temple setting.

However, at the end of this first day, the thing that seems to linger in our consciousness is the emphasis on families, especially between parents and children. Jesus prayed for the parents and blessed their children. Jesus's concern for families is reconfirmed when he told the multitude to "Pray in your families unto the Father, always in my name, that your wives and your children may be blessed" (3 Nephi 18:21). He then taught them how they should treat everyone, including transgressors, using the same language he had used in the Old World regarding little children: "suffer them that they may come unto you and forbid them not" (compare 3 Nephi 18:22 and Mark 10:14). This is what he did and continues to do for each of us—forbids us not to come to him, no matter what. No wonder he told the Nephites that he was the light that they should hold up (3 Nephi 18:24).

Furthermore, as Jesus ascended into heaven and the multitude dispersed for the evening, the record again impresses upon us the importance of families and what had occurred to families on that day: "Every man did take his wife and his children and did return to his own home" to prepare for the next day (3 Nephi 19:1; compare 17:3). Whether in temples or in the very presence of God himself, the importance of families is never to be overestimated. The Fifth Gospel helps us to see this.

Notes

1. John W. Welch, *Illuminating the Sermon at the Temple and Sermon on the Mount* (Provo, Utah: Foundation fo Ancient Research and Mormon Studies, 1999), 26.

2. Ibid., 226.

3. Bruce R. McConkie, *Doctrinal New Testament Commentary*, 3 vols. (Salt Lake City: Bookcraft, 1965), 1:708.

4. Joseph Smith, *Teachings of the Prophet Joseph Smith* (Salt Lake City: Deseret Book, 1977), 308–309; emphasis added.

5. *Journal of Discourses*, 26 vols. (London: Latter-day Saints' Book Depot, 1854–86), 10:241.

6. Omer Englebert, *A Short History of the Grotto of the Lord's Prayer*, (Jerusalem: Sisheb 1969), 5. He is quoting Eusebius: *Ecclesiastical History* III, 43; IV, 17.

7. Boyd K. Packer, "Teach the Children," *Ensign*, February 2000, 16–17.

8. Smith, *Teachings of the Prophet Joseph Smith*, 347, 361, 367.

9. Ibid., 324; emphasis added.

10. M. Russell Ballard, "Great Shall Be the Peace of Thy Children," *Ensign*, April 1994, 59.

11. John W. Welch was among the first to reach a similar conclusion. See his *Sermon at the Temple and Sermon on the Mount*, 98–99.

4

The Temple Sermon on Exaltation

ONE OF THE FIRST THINGS JESUS DID WHEN HE APPEARED TO THE Nephites at the temple in the land Bountiful was to present a slightly different version of the Sermon on the Mount given in the Old World. How appropriate it was for this sermon to be delivered at the temple. Its location was not an accident, for it is really a temple discourse. The ultimate purpose of the temple is to prepare people to enjoy eternal life, to live with Deity in the celestial kingdom. That is the ultimate purpose of the sermon as well. The sermon, both the Old and New World versions, is all about the nature and personal characteristics disciples must possess to live with God, and how such a person that possesses or desires to possess those qualities will live *in* the world but *not like* the world. Of course, it is easy to see today how the path to eternal life goes through the temple. I hope that after our discussion it will also be easy to see how the qualities, characteristics, doctrines, and concepts preached in the sermon at the temple are intricately bound up with the temple and thus why the temple was the perfect setting for Jesus's teachings.

TEMPLE SETTING

The setting for both the Sermon on the Mount and the sermon at the temple involved multitudes. In Palestine, Jesus attracted followers from all areas of his mortal ministry—Galilee, Decapolis, Jerusalem, Judea, and beyond Jordan. Therefore, "seeing the multitudes, he went up into a *mountain*" to teach (Matthew 5:1; emphasis added). In the land of Bountiful in the New World, the multitude was assembled "round about the *temple*" (3 Nephi 11:1; emphasis added). This is an impressive and important similarity, though it is perhaps not immediately apparent. While it has been argued persuasively that Jesus going up to the Galilean mount in Matthew's account paralleled the prophet Moses going up to Mount Sinai and receiving the law, the mountain setting of this sermon also evoked a powerful sense of going up to the temple to participate in worship, sacrifice, or instruction. The mountain-temple connection in ancient Israel is well established. A common Hebrew name for the Jerusalem temple was *har ha-bayit*, "mountain of the house." A good example comes from a passage well known to the Latter-day Saints, Isaiah 2:2, wherein the temple is called *har bēt Yahweh*, "the *mountain* of the Lord's house" (emphasis added). Latter-day Saint authorities have also referred to mountains as God's first temples.

Another connection between the sermon (both accounts) and the temple can be seen almost immediately in the very first section of the sermon, called the Beatitudes. Many, if not all, of the Beatitudes were based on Israel's ancient psalms, and the psalms were recognized as sacred songs or hymns rooted in the temple. One of the most prominent non-LDS experts on Israel's ancient psalms has emphasized that the psalms were centered in and an important part of Israelite and later Jewish temple worship.[1] An LDS authority on the Bible has stated flatly, "Many of the Psalms . . . though also sung at home or in the synagogue . . . were originally designed or later adapted for use in (or in connection with) the Temple."[2] Because several passages in the Beatitudes echo words and phrases from the psalms "that were particularly at home in the Temple,"[3] the Beatitudes, as well as the entire sermon, took on another added layer of temple-oriented meaning.

A good—perhaps the best—example of the three-fold link among the Beatitudes, the psalms, and the temple is seen in 3 Nephi 12:8 and in Matthew 5:8: "Blessed are the pure in heart, for they shall see God." That Jesus had in mind the temple as the foundation upon which this promise rests is seen in the direct parallel to Psalm 24, one of the psalms of ascent or procession sung by the Levites and priests as devotees went up to the Jerusalem temple to worship and participate in the sacrifices.[4] Part of this psalm reads:

Who shall ascend into the hill of the Lord? or who shall stand in his holy place?

He that hath clean hands, and *a pure heart*; who hath not lifted up his soul unto vanity, nor sworn deceitfully.

He shall receive the blessing from the Lord, and righteousness from the God of his salvation.

This is the generation of them . . . that seek thy face, O Jacob . . .

Who is this King of glory? The Lord of hosts, he is the King of glory. (Psalm 24:3–6, 10; emphasis added)

Though the King James Version (KJV) of Psalm 24 uses the words "hill of the Lord," the Hebrew is more directly related to the temple. "Who shall go up to the mountain of Yahweh" is a reference to the Lord's mountain house as we saw in Isaiah 2:2. And the phrase "who shall stand in his holy place" means nothing but the temple, since a section of the Jerusalem temple was explicitly called "the Holy Place." The implication of the KJV of Psalm 24 is that one could encounter God in the temple. The Septuagint version of this psalm (referred to as LXX in the Greek translation of the Old Testament) is even more explicit in pointing out that the ultimate intent of going up to the temple was to "seek the face of the God of Jacob":

Who shall go up to the mountain of the Lord, and who shall stand in his holy place?

He that is innocent in his hands and pure in his heart; who has not lifted up his soul to vanity, nor sworn deceitfully to his neighbor.

He shall receive a blessing from the Lord, and mercy from God his Saviour.

This is the generation of them that seek him, that seek the face of the God of Jacob . . .

Who is this king of glory? The Lord of hosts, he is this king of glory. (LXX Psalm 23:3–6, 10)

The Nephites would have been well aware of the link between the mountain of the Lord and the temple, even though they did not know of the Septuagint version of the Old Testament. And they certainly knew of the inseparable connection between purity in word and deed and the holiness requisite to enter the temple, which was the house of the Lord. Lehi and others may have even heard Psalm 24 being chanted at the temple sometime before they left Jerusalem.

Thus, Jesus was not contradicting Israelite or Jewish beliefs regarding the possibility of encountering God's presence in the temple if one had clean hands and a pure heart. Rather, he was developing, elevating, and emphasizing one of the most sacred and ennobling of Israelite beliefs. The righteous seeking after and seeing God in the temple is not an insignificant theme in the Old Testament and is perhaps best captured in other psalms of ancient Israel: "As for me, I will behold thy face in righteousness: I shall be satisfied, when I awake, with thy likeness" (Psalm 17:15). Also, "O God, thou art my God; early will I seek thee: my soul thirsteth for thee . . . To see thy power and thy glory, so as I have seen thee in the sanctuary [temple]" (Psalm 63:1–2).

In the literature of rabbinic Judaism—the Judaism of Jesus's day—the idea of entering God's presence in the temple reached something of an apex, wherein "one speaks of 'seeing God' in a dominant and literal sense; . . . one encounters the Shekhinah [the Divine Presence], when one arrives [in the temple], where God dwells in his mercy-presence in the Temple." [5] In the Beatitudes, Jesus broadened the opportunity to receive blessings formerly promised to the righteous in the temple by declaring that the purity required to see God in the temple was now asked of all true disciples, who could then see God without necessarily being in the temple in Jerusalem. True disciples thus live constantly in a virtual temple, where their holiness puts them ever before the Holy One. This actually has echoes of the theology of the covenanters living at Qumran (the Dead Sea Scroll community) during Jesus's day, whose objective was also to live their lives as if continuously in the temple.

It seems undeniable to me that the temple and the temple psalms served as the foundation for Jesus's instruction in the Sermon on the Mount and, likewise, his New World sermon at the temple. His intent in both versions was to teach temple-centered truths, the ultimate being that individuals must prepare on earth to live forever in heaven but can encounter the presence of God in mortality. In this regard, the New Testament sermon (Matthew 5–7) and the 3 Nephi sermon (3 Nephi 12–14) are cut of the same cloth.

CONTENT OF THE BEATITUDES

In both the Old and New World versions of his temple discourse, Jesus began by laying out a series of formulaic pronouncements called "beatitudes" because of the first word of each statement, which, in English, means "Blessed." That is, "Blessed are the meek, the merciful, the pure in heart [and so forth] . . ." In the Latin version of the New Testament, the word translated as "Blessed" is *beatus* (hence "beatitude"), which means "to be blessed, fortunate, happy." Those who cultivate and possess those characteristics outlined by Jesus in the Beatitudes will enjoy a blessed, joyous state for eternity.

The literary form of each of the Beatitudes is based on an ancient Hebraic form of speech, *'ashre*, well known in the Hebrew Bible (our Old Testament). In the Masoretic Text (the Hebrew text type on which the KJV is based), the term *'ashre* occurs forty-four times, the majority of which are in the Psalms. The very first psalm begins with it: *'Ashre ha'ish 'asher lo' halakh*—"Blessed is the man that walketh not [in the counsel of the ungodly]" (Psalm 1:1). Other examples are interesting because they help us to see that Jesus did not invent the form of instruction known as the Beatitudes. Rather, he was relying on an ancient Hebrew verbal construction, found more often than not in the Psalms, and always pointing out the type of behavior Deity expects from those who desire to become like God.

Consider the following in which *'ashre* is found: "*Blessed* are all who take refuge in [the Lord]" (Psalm 2:12); "*Blessed* is he whose transgression is forgiven, whose sin is covered. *Blessed* is the man to whom the Lord imputes no iniquity, and in whose spirit there is not deceit" (Psalm 32:1–2); "*Blessed* is the man who makes the Lord his trust, who does not turn to the proud" (Psalm 40:4); "*Blessed* is he who considers the poor" (Psalm 41:2); "*Blessed* are those who dwell in thy house" (Psalm 84:4); "*Blessed* are they who observe justice, who do righteousness at all times" (Psalm 106:3); "*Blessed* are those whose way is blameless, who walk in the law of the Lord. *Blessed* are those who keep his testimonies, who seek him with their whole heart" (Psalm 119:1–2); and "*Blessed* is every one who fears the Lord who walks in his ways" (Psalm 128:1).

The Beatitudes in the New Testament and in 3 Nephi constitute a list of characteristics, attributes, and blessings possessed by those who are striving for holiness and who are or shall be citizens of the kingdom of heaven. In the Beatitudes, we see that "Jesus is actually describing the qualities of an exalted person." [6] President Harold B. Lee said: "These declarations of the Master are known in the literature of the Christian world as the Beatitudes and have been referred to by Bible commentators as the preparation necessary for entrance into the kingdom of heaven. For the purposes of this discussion may I speak of them as something more than that as they are applied to you and me. They embody in fact the constitution for a perfect life."[7]

The Beatitudes also reflect the personalities—the makeup and qualities—of God the Father and his Son, Jesus Christ. Again, President Lee has noted that in the Sermon on the Mount, particularly the Beatitudes, "the Master has given us somewhat of a revelation of his own character, which was perfect, or what might be said to be 'an autobiography, every syllable of which he had written down in deeds,' and in so doing has given us a blueprint for our own lives."[8] And so at the end of the section in the sermon containing the Beatitudes, disciples are commanded to be perfect as our Father in Heaven is perfect, or as Nephi reports, "be perfect even as I, or your Father who is in heaven is perfect" (3 Nephi 12:48). This, arguably, is the capstone exhortation of the whole sermon as well as the Beatitudes. Put bluntly, the Beatitudes collectively are saying, "Blessed for eternity will be the person who possesses the characteristics that I and my Father possess."

It is interesting to note where the Beatitudes fit chronologically after Jesus initially appeared to the Nephites. First, he declared his role in the Atonement and invited the multitude to become personal witnesses of his resurrection. Next he taught "his doctrine," including the ordinance of baptism. And following that came this sermon on celestial living, which began with the Beatitudes. Surely its placement in the sequence of the Savior's three-day visit hints at the importance of the Beatitudes to him.

One cannot but help notice an immediate difference between the first beatitudes presented in the New World and those given in the Old World. In 3 Nephi, we read:

> He stretched forth his hand unto the multitude, and cried unto them, saying: *Blessed* are ye if ye shall give heed unto the words of these twelve whom I have chosen from among you to minister unto you, and to be your servants; and unto them I have given power that they may baptize you with water; and after that ye are baptized with water, behold, I will baptize you with fire and with the Holy Ghost; therefore *blessed* are ye if ye shall believe in me and be baptized, after that ye have seen me and know that I am.
>
> And again, more *blessed* are they who shall believe in your words because that ye shall testify that ye have seen me, and that ye know that I am. Yea, *blessed* are they who shall believe in your words, and come down into the depths of humility and be baptized, for they

shall be visited with fire and with the Holy Ghost, and shall receive a remission of their sins. (3 Nephi 12:1–2; emphasis added)

In this beginning statement, Jesus emphasized seven essential principles. First, he reminded his listeners that he had chosen twelve special ministers to whom he gave power and authority to baptize, and he promised those who follow them that they would be blessed. Second, he promised the multitude that they would be blessed if they would be baptized by those possessing authority given by him. Third, he promised all those who would be baptized would receive the gift of the Holy Ghost sent by the Savior (compare John 16:13). Fourth, he declared that members of the multitude had a responsibility to testify to others that they had literally "seen" the risen Lord. Fifth, he stated that those others would also be blessed if they too were baptized. Sixth, there is an important symbolic correlation between going "down into the depths of humility" and being baptized by proper authority. Seventh, he declared that all who are baptized with water and with fire, the Holy Ghost, will receive a remission of their sins. Thus we see that these initial unique beatitudes not found in the Sermon on the Mount, confirm that the Beatitudes were intended for those who heeded the words of prophets and became baptized members of the Lord's Church and not originally for everyone, even though the Beatitudes may set forth inspiring standards of belief and conduct that can be beneficial to all audiences.

A RESTORATION PERSPECTIVE

Because of the richer, fuller content of the Beatitudes in 3 Nephi, it is much easier to see how they constitute statements intended for baptized disciples seeking exaltation. This is also easier to see in light of the interpretive help provided by the latter-day revelations given through the Prophet Joseph Smith. Accordingly, in the 3 Nephi version it is not just the poor in spirit who are blessed eternally, but the poor in spirit *who come unto Christ* (3 Nephi 12:3; emphasis added). For those who seek after him, Jesus is able to make weak things become strong unto them (Ether 12:27). And how does someone come unto Christ continually? By perpetually offering a broken heart and contrite spirit (3 Nephi 9:19–20). Only as we truly come unto Christ will we be perfected. Perfection comes only in and through Christ (Moroni 10:32). Sometimes the only thing we *can* do is come unto Christ and ask through our tears of repentance to "take away our stain" (Alma 24:11). Thus, we see immediately what a great help it is to our quest for eternal life to have the more complete version of the Beatitudes available to us.

Another essential characteristic of those who seek exaltation has to do with mourning: And again, "Blessed are all they that mourn, for they shall be comforted" (3 Nephi 12:4). Of all the Beatitudes, this one may at first appear to be the most difficult to comprehend. Mourning seems contradictory to a state or condition of happiness or blessedness. To mourn is to show grief or pain at the loss of something precious, whether the death of a loved one or the loss of the Spirit of the Lord because of transgression. However, the Lord promised His disciples on another occasion that He would give rest and comfort to all who labored and were heavy laden if, again, they came unto Him (Matthew 11:28–30). As Elder Robert E. Wells has noted:

> It may be that pain and suffering at the death of loved ones is an essential part of our mortal experience that obliges us to face the question of the reality of the spirit world and the hope of the Resurrection. It is through suffering that we discover what is eternally important.
>
> It might be that it is a blessing for us to become more fully aware that God's ways are not always our ways, and that we must trust him when things don't go as we believe they should. When we can see the Lord's purposes fulfilled in our sorrowful moments, the Holy Ghost can console us and the Atonement and Resurrection can become the cornerstones of our faith.[9]

What is true about mourning over the loss of a loved one is also true about mourning over our sinful actions. "Godly sorrow," says Paul, "worketh repentance to salvation" (2 Corinthians 7:10). In other words, when we come unto Christ, we will become more sensitive to, and feel godly sorrow for, sin. His atonement becomes the cornerstone of our faith, and we continue to become more like Him as we repent.

The next beatitude centers on meekness. Because of a revelation given to Joseph Smith in 1832, called the "olive leaf," we now understand why "the meek shall inherit the earth" (3 Nephi 12:5). The meek are those who have followed the law of God and been resurrected with celestial bodies. This earth is destined to become the abode of those who inherit the celestial kingdom, and only those who are baptized may do so. The earth itself will be resurrected and become a celestial sphere. The Lord said,

And the resurrection from the dead is the redemption of the soul.

And the redemption of the soul is through him that quickeneth all things, in whose bosom it is decreed that the poor and the meek of the earth shall inherit it.

Therefore, it must needs be sanctified from all unrighteousness, that it may be prepared for the celestial glory;

For after it hath filled the measure of its creation, it shall be crowned with glory, even with the presence of God the Father;

That bodies who are of the celestial kingdom may possess it forever and ever; for, for this intent was it made and created, and for this intent are they sanctified.

And they who are not sanctified through the law which I have given unto you, even the law of Christ, must inherit another kingdom, even that of a terrestrial kingdom, or that of a telestial kingdom.

For he who is not able to abide the law of a celestial kingdom cannot abide a celestial glory. (D&C 88:16–22)

Another monumental addition to the Beatitudes is found in 3 Nephi 12:6. According to the Savior, those who hunger and thirst after righteousness will be filled—but filled with the Holy Ghost! How important it is to know this! It is the Holy Ghost who can give to us a testimony more sure than sight. It is the Holy Ghost who is the great comforter and testator and one of only three who can really satisfy our emotional and mental hunger and quench our spiritual thirst (John 14:16–18, 26). The Holy Ghost operates under the direction of Jesus Christ (John 16:13–16). The Greek word translated as "filled" and used by Matthew in his version of the sermon originally meant "to feed or fatten an animal in a stall" and carries the notion of eating till completely full, "to eat one's fill, be satisfied, to gorge." Such is the Lord's promise to those who hunger and thirst after righteousness. He will feed us more than we can imagine.

Through the Holy Ghost, we receive "the peaceable things of immortal glory; the truth of all things; that which quickeneth all things, which maketh alive all things; that which knoweth all things, and hath all power according to wisdom, mercy, truth, justice, and judgment" (Moses 6:61). It is the Holy Ghost whom the Father sends to teach us "all things" and bring "all things" to our remembrance (John 14:26). It is the Holy Ghost who can fill us with limitless power, as mortals measure power. Of the power possessed by the Holy Ghost, Elder James E. Talmage said:

The Holy Ghost may be regarded as the minister of the Godhead, carrying into effect the decisions of the Supreme Council.

In the execution of these great purposes, the Holy Ghost directs and controls the varied forces of nature, of which indeed a few, and these perhaps of minor order wonderful as even the least of them appears to man, have thus far been investigated by mortals. Gravitation, sound, heat, light, and the still more mysterious and seemingly supernatural power of electricity, are but the common servants of the Holy Ghost in His operations. No earnest thinker, no sincere investigator supposes that he has yet learned of all the forces existing in and operating upon matter; indeed, the observed phenomena of nature, yet wholly inexplicable to him, far outnumber those for which he has devised even a partial explanation. There are powers and forces at the command of God, compared with which electricity is as the pack-horse to the locomotive, the foot messenger to the telegraph, the raft of logs to the ocean steamer. With all his scientific knowledge man knows but little respecting the enginery of creation; and yet the few forces known to him have brought about miracles and wonders, which but for their actual realization would be beyond belief. These mighty agencies, and the mightier ones still to man unknown, and many, perhaps, to the present condition of the human mind unknowable, do not constitute the Holy Ghost, but are the agencies ordained to serve His purposes.[10]

OTHER CHANGES TO THE BEATITUDES

In the sermon at the temple, as in the Sermon on the Mount, the Savior spoke about mercy: "blessed are the merciful, for they shall obtain mercy" (3 Nephi 12:7). This beatitude has a special connection to Israel's ancient psalms. Many are the psalms that describe God's mercy. But here the issue is not that God is full of mercy but that his followers can obtain his mercy and the tangible results of his mercy because of the mercy they demonstrate toward others. As the Psalmist said, "The righteous sheweth mercy. . . . For such as be blessed of him shall inherit the earth" (Psalm 37:21–22; emphasis added). Thus, according to Psalm 37, both the meek (verse 11) and the merciful inherit the earth. Mercy seems to be a defining characteristic of true followers of him who is the source of eternal mercy through the Atonement. The merciful are drawn inextricably to the Merciful One, for mercy is a characteristic that is attracted to itself. As the Lord said, "For intelligence cleaveth unto intelligence; wisdom receiveth wisdom; truth embraceth truth; virtue loveth virtue; light cleaveth unto light; mercy hath compassion on mercy and claimeth her own; justice continueth its course and claimeth its own; judgment goeth before the face of him who sitteth upon the throne and governeth and executeth all things" (D&C 88:40; emphasis added). The rabbis of Jesus's day believed in that concept: "He who shows mercy to his fellow creature obtains mercy from Heaven."[11] Therefore, the Psalmist indicates that the merciful are drawn to the house of the Merciful One, the temple: "But as for me, I will come into thy house in the multitude of thy mercy: and in thy fear will I worship toward thy holy temple" (Psalm 5:7).

The greatest act of mercy ever performed was the selfless sacrifice of the Son of God. Because he gave his life as an offering to appease the demands of justice, each of us will live again and have the opportunity for an exalted eternal existence. Jesus's personal sacrifice gives him the right and the power to forgive us and plead our cause before our Father in Heaven (D&C 45:3–5). When we act toward others as the Savior has acted toward us, we become like him and our merciful behavior welds us to him. A corollary of the message in this beatitude on mercy is forgiveness. As Jesus said later in the sermon, "For, if ye forgive men their trespasses your heavenly Father will also forgive you; but if ye forgive not men their trespasses neither will your Father forgive your trespasses" (3 Nephi 13:14–15).

In the beatitude describing the reward of peacemakers (3 Nephi 12:9), Jesus tied together the doctrine of adoption and the concept of peacemaking. To be called God's children in the fullest sense, disciples must first do what Jesus does, act as he acts. Jesus is the Prince of Peace (see Isaiah 9:6); therefore his disciples also must be peacemakers. As disciples imitate Jesus and obey him, they are spiritually adopted into his family and become his children (see Mosiah 5:7). Adoption as Jesus Christ's children leads to full inheritance of all that God the Father has and all that he is. The Apostle Paul illuminates our understanding of the full meaning of adoption: "The Spirit itself beareth witness with your spirit, that we are the children of God: and if children, then heirs; heirs of God, and joint-heirs with Christ; if so be that we suffer with him, that we may be also glorified together" (Romans 8:16–17).

Christ is the only natural Son of God and heir to kingship. However, through adoption made possible by the Atonement, disciples also become the children of God and heirs of all that the Father has to give: "Those who are sons [and daughters] of God in this sense are the ones who become gods in the world to come (D&C 76:54–60). They have exaltation and godhood because the family unit continues in eternity (D&C 132:19–24) . . . Through Christ and his atoning sacrifice they are 'begotten sons and daughters unto God' (D&C 76:24), meaning the Father." [12]

Last but not least among the Beatitudes are the promises made to those who are persecuted for the cause of righteousness (3 Nephi 12:10–11). But note the difference between the version in Matthew 5:10–11 and the one in 3 Nephi. To the disciples in the Old World, he said: "Blessed are they which are persecuted *for righteousness' sake.*" To his New World Israelites, he declared, "blessed are all they who are persecuted *for my name's sake*" (3 Nephi 12:10). It has been argued that when Jesus extolled the blessed state of those who were persecuted for righteousness' sake (Matthew 5:10), he was really saying "for the sake of *the Righteous One*"—meaning himself.[13] This is the meaning found in 3 Nephi. In Hebrew, the difference between *zedeq* (righteousness) and *zadiq* (righteous one) is very small. Either way, disciples are bid to follow Jesus because he is the Righteous One and the embodiment of righteousness. Persecution was the path the Master himself trod: "If they have persecuted me, they will also persecute you" (John 15:20). This persecution culminated on the Cross.

The reward promised to the disciples who would take upon themselves Jesus's name was the kingdom of heaven. The disciples could take heart in knowing that they were following the path of the great ones before them, "for so persecuted they the prophets which were before you" (3 Nephi 12:12).

A modern revelation received by President Joseph F. Smith in 1918 confirms and expands the promise made by Jesus to all those who suffer persecution for their Redeemer's name—the promise of a place in the kingdom of heaven.

> As I pondered over these things which are written, the eyes of my understanding were opened, and the Spirit of the Lord rested upon me, and I saw the hosts of the dead, both small and great.
> And there were gathered together in one place an innumerable company of the spirits of the just, who had been faithful in the testimony of Jesus while they lived in mortality;
> And who had offered sacrifice in the similitude of the great sacrifice of the Son of God, and had suffered tribulation in their Redeemer's name. (D&C 138:11–13)

No greater reward could be promised to anyone than the kingdom of heaven. The promises made in the Beatitudes and the promises made in God's temples culminate with life in the kingdom of heaven.

REMAINDER OF THE SERMON

After presenting the Beatitudes, Jesus went on to speak of other qualities that celestial-bound disciples should possess and demonstrate in a fallen, corrupt world, yet with their sights elevated toward the glory of heaven. As the salt of the earth (3 Nephi 12:13), they would be recognized by their covenants, since salt is a symbol of the covenant men make with God (Numbers 18:19; 2 Chronicles 13:5). Just as salt does not lose its savor with age—only through mixture and contamination with other substances—followers of Christ are warned to avoid the corrupting influences of the world. They must remain pure and undefiled. They are to be the light unto others (3 Nephi 12:14–16) just as their Master is the light of the world (John 8:12).

A rather striking section of the sermon at the temple (see 3 Nephi 12:19–45) contains several cautions about personal behavior that warn listeners to look beyond the mere written, outward prohibitions of the law of Moses and act according to the higher dictates of a changed heart, which every true follower of Christ will possess (Mosiah 5:2; Alma 5:12–14). These are easily recognized by their formulaic construction: "Ye have heard that it hath been said by them of old time . . . But I say unto . . ." (3 Nephi 12:27–28). The principle Jesus was trying to teach the people was that the old Mosaic dispensation was done away with, and the new Gospel dispensation, restored in their day, would lead *all* men and women to a state of perfection and exaltation. A summary declaration describes this aspect of the gospel message: "Therefore those things which were of old time, which were under the law, in me are all fulfilled. Old things are done away, and all things have become new. Therefore I would that ye should be perfect even as I, or your Father who is in heaven is perfect" (3 Nephi 12:46–48).

Perfection is the objective of every saint—nothing less. It can only be gained through Jesus Christ. All who achieve it will be just like the Father and the Son. Great expectations produce great blessings. Yet, at the conclusion of the sermon at the temple, there were still some who wondered how the law of Moses should be regarded. The Savior explained in no uncertain terms that he was Jehovah, the giver of the Law, and that the law was now fulfilled because he said so. Perhaps no other passage of scripture declares so forcefully Jesus's premortal identity as Jehovah and redirects souls to Jesus Christ.

> And it came to pass that when Jesus had said these words he perceived that there were some among them who marveled, and wondered what he would concerning the law of Moses; for they understood not the saying that old things had passed away, and that all things had become new.
>
> And he said unto them: Marvel not that I said unto you that old things had passed away, and that all things had become anew.
>
> Behold, I say unto you that the law is fulfilled that was given unto Moses.
>
> Behold, I am he that gave the law, and I am he who covenanted with my people Israel; therefore, the law in me is fulfilled, for I have come to fulfil the law; therefore it hath an end . . .
>
> For behold, the covenant which I have made with my people is not all fulfilled; but the law which was given unto Moses hath an end in me.
>
> Behold, I am the law, and the light. Look unto me, and endure to the end, and ye shall live; for unto him that endureth to the end will I give eternal life. (3 Nephi 15:2–5, 8–9)

KNOWLEDGE OF THE FATHER

The sermon at the temple speaks much about our Father in Heaven. In the sermon, Jesus brought God the Father back into focus through a series of parables, commands, and explanations.

Perhaps the greatest attribute of God the Father is love. The Apostle John wrote, "God is love" (1 John 4:8). We can assume he meant that perfect love and fairness always direct, shape, mediate, and influence all of God's other attributes, "for with all the other excellencies in his character, without this one to influence them, they could not have such powerful dominion over the minds of men." [14] Thus, in the sermon at the temple, Jesus commands His audience to love their enemies, bless those who curse them, and pray for those who spitefully use them. Why? "That ye may be the children of your Father which is in heaven" (3 Nephi 12:45).

The Greek wording of Matthew 5:45, the parallel to 3 Nephi 12:45, connotes a rebirth of sorts: "so that you may become [be born] (*genēsthe*) sons of your Father in heaven." This idea parallels the doctrine of being spiritually born of God and receiving his image in one's countenance, as found in Alma 5:14. Disciples must reflect in their lives, in their behaviors, and in their countenances the distinguishing trait of the great Parent of the universe in order to truly become his children and his heirs.

God the Father loves all his children, even those who forsake or ignore him. He is patient and long-suffering, and "he maketh his sun to rise on the evil and on the good" (3 Nephi 12:45), meaning that righteousness and wickedness cannot be immediately and constantly rewarded or punished. Such constant interference in the lives of men and women would thwart the plan of salvation and the purposes for which earth life was designed—to allow individuals to walk by faith and be tested. It is no accident that Jesus concludes this section of the Sermon by commanding his listeners to be perfect as their Father in heaven is perfect (3 Nephi 12:48). Patient love and tolerant restraint are the great hallmarks of God's perfection, but they are also the Savior's, as the Savior indicated.

Jesus spent a good deal of the next portion of his sermon teaching about the nature of our Father in heaven by discussing private daily devotions. Do not, he said, make a public show of doing that which is better done privately—almsgiving, welfare relief, and personal prayer (3 Nephi 13:1–6)—for "thy Father, who seeth in secret shall reward thee openly" (3 Nephi 13:6). Those who give alms to be seen of men are "hypocrites," an epithet used to describe people who sought prestige above all else. Because of Jesus's use of vocabulary such as "hypocrite" (Greek, literally "play actor, pretender, dissembler"), some authorities see this as evidence to connect the mortal Jesus with visits to theatre towns such as Sepphoris, only a few miles north of Nazareth.[15] While Jesus may not have used the Greek word with his American Israelites, whatever term he did use certainly conveyed the same meaning.

As the sermon progressed, Jesus continued to emphasize that God the Father cares about proper decorum. His is a kingdom of quiet dignity, and he honors those who behave in like manner. He prefers brevity, sincerity, and intensity in prayer, unlike the "heathen" (in Matthew, Greek, *ethnikoi*, literally "Gentiles") who use "vain repetitions" (Greek, *battalogēsēte*, literally "babble," or "speaking without thinking") and "think that they shall be heard for their much speaking" (3 Nephi 13:7).

Such ideas as Jesus presented correspond, in a remarkable way, to the ideas on prayer as expressed in Jewish rabbinic thought. Rabbi Simeon said, "Be careful in reading the Shema [the Jewish confession of faith found in Deuteronomy 6:4–7] . . . . [For] when you pray, do not regard your prayer as a perfunctory act (or fixed form), but as a plea for mercy and grace before God, as it is said: 'For he is gracious and merciful, slow to anger, abounding in kindness, and relenting of evil.' " [16]

Following his instruction on prayer, Jesus presented a series of doctrinal statements that tell his disciples much more about our Heavenly Father's personality and desires for his sons and daughters. For example, God is forgiving, but he requires that individuals forgive each other or his divine mercy will be held in abeyance (3 Nephi 13:14–15). God rewards those who fast with dignity, not with outward showiness and not seeking sympathy (3 Nephi 13:16–18). Where our heart is, what we think about and act on, is what we value most. Therefore, we should work toward that which is the most important from an eternal perspective—and it isn't money. No one can seek riches (*mammon*) wholeheartedly and serve God with the same intensity. In other words, no one can keep one foot in the world and the other in the kingdom and expect to inherit eternal life. It is impossible. Mortality is entirely about showing where our loyalty truly rests.

Ultimately, said Jesus, if one's eye—one's attitudes, priorities, and motives—were "single," his or her whole body would be full of light. This is exactly what the Lord revealed to Joseph Smith: "And if your eye be single to my glory, your whole bodies shall be filled with light, and there shall be no darkness in you; and that body which is filled with light comprehendeth all things" (D&C 88:67). Through single-minded focus on God's will and God's glory, Jesus's disciples could reap an incredible reward—being filled with light, truth, and comprehension of all things. But anything other than single-minded focus on God would dissipate the light and increase the darkness (3 Nephi 13:23). Jesus himself was and is the Great Exemplar. With his whole soul, he concentrated on doing the will of his Father. As a result, he was filled with light; he was the Light of the World. In almost everything Jesus taught, his underlying message was, "if you act like me, you will become like me, and to become like me is also to become like God the Father."

CONCLUSION

In the last section of the sermon at the temple, like the Sermon on the Mount, Jesus changed the focus of his instruction and specifically turned his attention to training the Twelve he had chosen to lead his American Israelites (3 Nephi 13:25–14:27). This is made so much clearer in 3 Nephi than in Matthew's version of the sermon, owing to Moroni's very helpful observation: "And now it came to pass that when Jesus had spoken these words he looked upon the twelve whom he had chosen, and said unto them: Remember the words which I have spoken. For behold, ye are they whom I have chosen to minister unto this people" (3 Nephi 13:25).

Part of the content of this latter instruction we will take up in the next chapters. Suffice it to say that no mortal man has ever preached a discourse like the sermon at the temple. It was shaped by the place where it was delivered—the temple. And it was filled with doctrine that leads to exaltation; it describes the characteristics that the exalted will possess in the eternities and must display in mortality. It describes the very personality of Jesus Christ. It invites all to come to him and thus to become exactly like him. Its teachings carry the force of commandments; and it is quite unequivocal in its directive—follow the sermon and be saved, or ignore it and be damned in our eternal progress. "Therefore," says the Savior in the sermon, "come unto me and be saved; for verily I say unto you, that except ye shall keep my commandments, which I have commanded you at this time, ye shall in no case enter into the kingdom" (3 Nephi 12:20).

The sermon delivered at the temple will help disciples, ancient or modern, to build a sure and certain spiritual foundation. And this is precisely the point with which the Savior concluded his remarks:

> Therefore, whoso heareth these sayings of mine and doeth them, I will liken him unto a wise man, who built his house upon a rock—
>
> And the rain descended, and the floods came, and the winds blew, and beat upon that house; and it fell not, for it was founded upon a rock.
>
> And every one that heareth these sayings of mine and doeth them not shall be likened unto a foolish man, who built his house upon the sand—
>
> And the rain descended, and the floods came, and the winds blew, and beat upon that house; and it fell, and great was the fall of it. (3 Nephi 14:24–27)

NOTES

1. Sigmund Mowinckel, *The Psalms in Israel's Worship* (New York: Abingdon, 1962), 2:89–90.

2. John W. Welch, *The Sermon on the Mount in the Light of the Temple* (Surrey, England: Ashgate, 2009), 43.

3. Ibid.

4. George A. Buttrick, ed. *The Interpreter's Bible* (Nashville: Abingdon, 1978), 4:131, 133.

5. Welch, *Sermon on the Mount in Light of the Temple*, 55.

6. Church Educational System, *The Life and Teachings of Jesus and His Apostles* (Salt Lake City: The Church of Jesus Christ of Latter-day Saints, 1978), 60.

7. Harold B. Lee, *Decisions for Successful Living* (Salt Lake City: Deseret Book, 1973), 57.

8. Ibid., 56.

9. Robert E. Wells, "Pattern for Coming unto Christ," *Ensign*, December 1987, 9.

10. James E. Talmage, *Articles of Faith*, 48th ed. (Salt Lake City: The Church of Jesus Christ of Latter-day Saints, 1967), 160–61.

11. Samuel T. Lachs, *A Rabbinic Commentary on the New Testament* (Hoboken, NJ: KTAV, 1987), 75.

12. Bruce R. McConkie, *Doctrinal New Testament Commentary*, 3 vols. (Salt Lake City: Bookcraft, 1965–71), 2:474–75.

13. Lachs, *A Rabbinic Commentary on the New Testament*, 77.

14. Joseph Smith, *Lectures on Faith* (Salt Lake City: Deseret Book, 1985), 3:24.

15. Richard A. Batey, *Jesus and the Forgotten City: New Light on Sephoris and the Urban World of Jesus* (Grand Rapids: Baker, 1991), 83–103.

16. *Pirqe Avot* 2:18 in Birnbaum, Daily Prayer Book (Hebrew Publishing Company: New York, 1977), 490.

5

Apostolic Authority among Joseph's Remnant

Recognized priesthood authority has always been a crucial component of the Lord's true Church. Among the very first acts performed by the Savior during his New World ministry was the establishment of Church leadership with authority to perform ordinances.

Calling the Twelve in the New World

Immediately after he descended out of heaven, having declared his Messianic identity, Jesus called for Nephi to come forth from the crowd in order to give him power to baptize—the first of twelve such ministers (3 Nephi 11:18, 21–22). It must have been an overwhelming moment for Nephi, since twenty-five hundred people looked on. Nephi stood, approached the Savior, bowed down, and kissed the feet of God! What an incredible sight. Nephi's action obviously represented a supreme gesture of love, loyalty, and humility.

The other Gospels record instances in which disciples in the Old World acted similarly. When a certain Pharisee named Simon invited Jesus to have dinner, a woman who had lived a sinful life found out that Jesus was dining in the man's house. She went to the house with an alabaster jar of perfume, "And stood at [Jesus's] feet behind him weeping, and began to wash his feet with tears, and did wipe them with the hairs of her head, and kissed his feet, and anointed them with the ointment" (Luke 7:38).

During the last week of his mortal existence, Jesus went to Bethany and had supper with his close friends Martha, Mary, and Lazarus. "Then took Mary a pound of ointment of spikenard, very costly, and anointed the feet of [the Anointed One], and wiped his feet with her hair" (John 12:3).

Perhaps more impressive, we know certain women had gone to the Sepulchre to pay their respects on the first Easter morn. They ended up leaving an open, empty tomb with fear and great joy to go and tell the disciples that their Master had risen from the dead. "And as they went . . . behold, Jesus met them, saying, All hail. And they came and held him by the feet, and worshipped him" (Matthew 28:9). To bow at the Savior's feet, feet which bore the emblems of his atoning sacrifice, is a well-recognized gesture of worship, as the Gospels testify. To these remarkable accounts, we may add Nephi's sublime act.

In modern times, a modern Apostle, Elder Bruce R. McConkie, spoke prophetically in general conference of his own anticipated Nephi-like experience in front of the Savior. It was just days before his death; he was suffering from the ravages of disease, and the effects of his words were profoundly moving. He said: "I am one of his witnesses, and in a coming day I shall feel the nail marks in his hands and in his feet and shall wet his feet with my tears. But I shall not know any better then than I know now that he is God's Almighty Son, that he is our Savior and Redeemer, and that salvation comes in and through his atoning blood and in no other way." [1] Nephi was a special witness; Elder McConkie was a special witness. Their two testimonies anchor each other and span the gap of two millennia.

Following Nephi's encounter with the risen Lord, he "called others and said unto them likewise; and gave unto them power to baptize. And he said unto them: On this wise shall ye baptize; and there shall be no disputations among you" (3 Nephi 11:22). It seems obvious at first that what Jesus intended by counseling these men that there should be "no disputations among you" was to forestall any alternative proposals on who had authority to baptize or the method by which it was to be done. He repeated this instruction a few verses later: "And according as I have commanded you thus shall ye baptize. And there shall be no disputations among you, as there have hitherto been; neither shall there be disputations among you concerning the points of my doctrine, as there have hitherto been" (3 Nephi 11:28). Jesus also gave similar counsel when instructing these leaders on the administration of the sacrament (3 Nephi 18:34).

However, something else may also be seen here. When Jesus was setting up his church in this last dispensation, he gave a commandment to Church leaders at a conference in 1831 regarding their relationship to one another. He said:

> And let every man esteem his brother as himself, and practise virtue and holiness before me.
>
> And again I say unto you, let every man esteem his brother as himself.
>
> For what man among you having twelve sons, and is no respecter of them, and they serve him obediently, and he saith unto the one: Be thou clothed in robes and sit thou here; and to the other: Be thou clothed in rags and sit thou there—and looketh upon his sons and saith I am just?
>
> Behold, this I have given unto you as a parable, and it is even as I am. I say unto you, be one; and if ye are not one ye are not mine. (D&C 38:24–27)

It seems significant to me that along with authority to perform the ordinance of baptism and information on how to baptize, the most fundamental piece of instruction Jesus gave to the Twelve in the New World was a commandment to be unified. We gain further insight into why Jesus emphasized unity among the Twelve in the New World in a revelation he gave to Joseph Smith in 1831. He mentioned a grave problem that had surfaced among the ancient disciples: "My disciples, in days of old, sought occasion against one another and forgave not one another in their hearts; and for this evil they were afflicted and sorely chastened" (D&C 64:8). Disunity, contention, and animosity, spurred on by the absence of charity, are the great roadblocks to progress on perfection's path. Unity had to be the foundation from which the disciples operated if they were going to lead the Church as Jesus led it. Jesus was one with his Father—a truth he proclaimed when the remnant of the people first heard his voice after the destruction of their land (3 Nephi 9:15)—and he proclaimed this doctrine again and again as the Twelve were being instructed.

Priesthood Authority

After Jesus had called the Twelve, he certified their authority and standing to the multitude as he began to deliver his sermon at the temple

(3 Nephi 12:1). It is clear that they were to be the guardians and keepers of doctrine as well as the sacred ordinances. They were to lead the people and bear witness of Jesus Christ as the resurrected Messiah and Son of God.

It is sometimes asked if the Twelve in the Western Hemisphere were Apostles, the reasoning being, I suppose, that there can only be one set of Twelve on earth at a time, and there was already a Quorum of the Twelve in the Old World. First, the Savior himself referred to them as "mine apostles" (Moroni 2:2). Second, the Prophet Joseph Smith included an important paragraph in what has come to be known as the Wentworth letter (which also contained the Articles of Faith for the first time). When speaking of the Book of Mormon in the letter he said:

> This book also tells us that our Savior made His appearance upon this continent after His resurrection; that He planted the Gospel here in all its fullness, and richness, and power, and blessing; that they had Apostles, Prophets, Pastors, Teachers, and Evangelists; the same order, the same priesthood, the same ordinances, gifts, powers, and blessings, as were enjoyed on the eastern continent, that the people were cut off in consequence of their transgressions, that the last of their prophets who existed among them was commanded to write an abridgment of their prophecies, history, &c, and to hide it up in the earth, and that it should come forth and be united with the Bible for the accomplishment of the purposes of God in the last days.[2]

According to the Prophet, things were not different for the Nephites than for us. The Church in the New World was organized like the Church in the Old World, and like the Church of Jesus Christ in our day, with various offices including Apostles and others with which we are familiar.

Third, subsequent modern prophet-leaders of the LDS Church have corroborated that the Nephite Twelve *were* Apostles. President Joseph Fielding Smith indicated that although the Nephite Twelve were called disciples, they were special witnesses of Christ and as such "the Nephite twelve became apostles."[3] Their jurisdiction was ultimately subject to the Twelve Apostles in Palestine, but they officiated in an apostolic ministry.[4]

All those who possessed priesthood power in the Western Hemisphere, including the Twelve Apostles chosen by Jesus, operated under the authority of the Melchizedek Priesthood from the time Lehi left Jerusalem until the coming of Jesus Christ. The Nephites (and Lamanites) were descendants of Joseph, part of the house, or family, of Israel. There were no Levites who accompanied Lehi and his family to the New World, and all priesthood they possessed was Melchizedek in nature because only the descendants of Levi could hold the Levitical or Aaronic Priesthood. Lehi, Nephi, Jacob, and others who succeeded them were prophets and Joseph Smith taught that all the prophets held the Melchizedek Priesthood.[5]

It is sometimes pointed out that Nephi "did consecrate Jacob and Joseph, that they should be priests and teachers over the land of [the Nephites]" (2 Nephi 5:26). However, these terms were used in a generic sense and not as specific offices in the lesser priesthood. Jacob's comment helps us to understand what priesthood he and his brother Joseph held: "Behold, my beloved brethren, I, Jacob, having been called of God, and ordained after the manner of *his holy order*, and having been consecrated by my brother Nephi" (2 Nephi 6:2; emphasis added). The phrase "his holy order" refers to the higher or Melchizedek Priesthood, as we learn from Alma 13:1–7 and Doctrine and Covenants 107:1–4. President Joseph Fielding Smith provides a significant and helpful statement that complements our discussion:

> When the Savior came to the Nephites, he established the Church in its fullness among them, and he informed them that former things had passed away, for they were all fulfilled in him. He gave the Nephites all the authority of the priesthood which we exercise today. Therefore we are justified in the belief that not only was the fulness of the Melchizedek Priesthood conferred, but also the Aaronic, just as we have it in the Church today; and this Aaronic Priesthood remained with them from this time until, through wickedness, all priesthood ceased. We may be assured that in the days of Moroni the Nephites did ordain teachers and priests in the Aaronic Priesthood; but before the visit of the Savior they officiated in the Melchizedek Priesthood.[6]

TRAINING THE TWELVE

Instruction to the Twelve on the first day of Jesus's visit initially emphasized the doctrine of Christ. This is one of the additions in the Fifth Gospel that gives it superior authority over the New Testament Gospels. Jesus summarized this doctrine powerfully:

> Behold, verily, verily, I say unto you, I will declare unto you my doctrine.

And this is my doctrine, and it is the doctrine which the Father hath given unto me; and I bear record of the Father, and the Father beareth record of me, and the Holy Ghost beareth record of the Father and me; and I bear record that the Father commandeth all men, everywhere, to repent and believe in me.

And whoso believeth in me, and is baptized, the same shall be saved; and they are they who shall inherit the kingdom of God.

And whoso believeth not in me, and is not baptized, shall be damned.

Verily, verily, I say unto you, that this is my doctrine, and I bear record of it from the Father; and whoso believeth in me believeth in the Father also; and unto him will the Father bear record of me, for he will visit him with fire and with the Holy Ghost. (3 Nephi 11:31–35)

Long explanations of this text seem unnecessary. It is simple but profound. The Savior emphasized five doctrines:

1. the Father, Son, and Holy Ghost bear record of each other;
2. the Father commands all persons everywhere to have faith in Christ and repent;
3. those who believe in Christ will be baptized and inherit the kingdom of God, while those who are not baptized will be damned;
4. whoever believes will receive the Holy Ghost; and
5. the previous four doctrines constitute the doctrine of Christ and whoever builds his or her life on this foundation will be preserved even though the gates of hell will try to prevail against them. The latter promise is majestic and powerful yet fundamental, and lends clarity to all of our discussions about the purpose of the gospel of Jesus Christ.

The doctrine of Christ embodies the first principles and ordinances of the Gospel. This is what the New World Apostles were to teach. To these first four principles and ordinances, Jesus added another for his American Israelites to follow: "for unto him that endureth to the end will I give eternal life" (3 Nephi 15:9). Enduring to the end is a necessary behavior pattern for Saints of the latter days to adopt. A significant tool given to all disciples to help them endure to the end is the temple endowment. The endowment gives us the ongoing motivation and the power to endure. Through the ordinance of the endowment, we are introduced to the environment of heaven, shown that it is within our grasp, and given the power to obtain it. The endowment truly is, as its name indicates, a rich gift.

That is another reason why the temple is critical to all we do. Given the emphasis the Savior placed on the "doctrine of Christ," I wonder if we spend enough time thinking and speaking about it and if we perhaps spend too much time on so-called "deeper" doctrines.

Having outlined the doctrine of Christ, Jesus then delivered the sermon at the temple. A significant portion of the sermon was directed specifically to the Twelve, as we have already noted, and served as something of an "MTC experience" for them (akin to instruction sessions given to missionaries today in the missionary training centers around the world). As a part of this special training, Jesus commanded the Twelve to *remember* the words he spoke to them (3 Nephi 13:25). Modern prophets have told us that "remember" is the most important word in our spiritual vocabulary. It was made even more poignant to the Twelve when Jesus emphasized the great responsibility that rested with them, for, said he, "ye are they whom *I have chosen* to minister unto this people" (3 Nephi 13:25; emphasis added). This parallels the charge given by Jesus to the Apostles in the Old World: "Ye have not chosen me, but I have chosen you, and ordained you" (John 15:16).

Other instruction to the New World Apostles centered on financial and subsistence issues. They were to take no thought for their personal welfare, but to concentrate wholly on building and shepherding the kingdom. "But seek ye first the kingdom of God and his righteousness, and all these things shall be added unto you" (3 Nephi 13:33). Jesus testified that Heavenly Father knew their needs and would care for them. They were not even to worry about future problems. He said, "Take therefore no thought for the morrow, for the morrow shall take thought for the things of itself. Sufficient is the day unto the evil thereof" (3 Nephi 13:34).

In other words, do not become anxiety-ridden over what might happen tomorrow. Each day brings enough trouble of its own without bringing on extra by worrying about what *might* happen. This is good advice for every member of the Church today, regardless of calling or position. It's okay to try to plan but excessive concern for the future can destroy us—reduce us to nervous wrecks. Much must be left to God. There is an old Jewish saying that teaches a profound lesson: "Men plan and God laughs" (it rhymes in Yiddish). If we spend all our time thinking about the *future*, we rob ourselves of what could be a rich and vibrant *present*. We must have faith in God and go forward into the future. President Thomas A. Monson declared, "The future is as bright as your faith." [7]

OTHER SHEEP

The third Gospel describes how Jesus alternated the focus of his teaching between the multitude in general and then the Twelve Apostles specifically. Chapter fifteen, for example, begins, "And now it came to pass that when Jesus had ended these sayings he cast his eyes round about on the multitude, and said unto them . . ." (3 Nephi 15:1). A few verses later, we are told, "And now it came to pass that when Jesus had spoken these words, he said unto those twelve whom he had chosen. . ." (3 Nephi 15:11). In this regard, the Fifth Gospel is much clearer than the four New Testament Gospels.

As Jesus continued his training of the Twelve, he commanded them to be a light unto their people. The land they occupied in the Western Hemisphere was their land of inheritance since they were a remnant of the house of Joseph (3 Nephi 15:12–13). This harks back to the patriarchal blessing that father Jacob (Israel) gave to Joseph in early Old Testament times. He pronounced the following blessing upon his son Joseph: "Joseph is a fruitful bough, even a fruitful bough by a well; whose branches run over the wall: . . . Even by the God of thy father, who shall help thee; and by the Almighty, who shall bless thee with blessings of heaven above, blessings of the deep that lieth under, blessings of the breasts, and of the womb: The blessings of thy father have prevailed above the blessings of my progenitors unto the utmost bound of the everlasting hills: they shall be on the head of Joseph, and on the crown of the head of him that was separate from his brethren" (Genesis 49:22, 25–26).

The "branches" of Joseph by a well, that "run over the wall," present the image of a large tree spreading beyond the land where it was originally planted into another part of the earth (verse 24). These branches, which symbolize the descendants of Joseph, would then receive greater blessings than Joseph's progenitors, even "unto the utmost bounds of the everlasting hills"—the Americas (verse 26). Elder Orson Pratt said that he supposed Jacob saw this land of America in vision when he pronounced his blessing.[8] The posterity of Joseph came to the lands of America when Lehi and his family left Jerusalem. The Twelve in the New World were being told they and their people were now realizing the promised blessings given to them from the Father through their earthly fathers, Jacob and Joseph. But, said the Savior, this information was privileged: "And not at any time hath the Father given me commandment that I should tell it unto your brethren at Jerusalem. Neither at any time hath the Father given me commandment that I should tell unto them concerning the other tribes of the house of Israel, whom the Father hath led away out of the land" (3 Nephi 15:14–15).

In other words, for a wise purpose the disciples in Jerusalem were not to know of their cousins, the American Israelites, or the other tribes who the Father had led away. The Old World disciples were given a brief allusion to other Israelites not found among them when Jesus said he had other sheep not of the flock in the Old World. But they were given nothing more than that, and the comment was undoubtedly viewed as cryptic (John 10:14–16). Elder James E. Talmage states that "the Jewish apostles had wrongly supposed that those 'other sheep' were the Gentile nations, not realizing that the carrying of the gospel to the Gentiles was part of their particular mission, and oblivious to the fact that never would Christ manifest Himself in person to those who were not of the house of Israel."[9] Now the Twelve in the New World were allowed to know that they were the fulfillment of Jesus's declaration in the Old World regarding his other sheep. Said Jesus to those twelve ministers:

> And verily I say unto you, that ye are they of whom I said: Other sheep I have which are not of this fold; them also I must bring, and they shall hear my voice; and there shall be one fold, and one shepherd.
> And they understood me not, for they supposed it had been the Gentiles; for they understood not that the Gentiles should be converted through their preaching.
> And they understood me not that I said they shall hear my voice; and they understood me not that the Gentiles should not at any time hear my voice—that I should not manifest myself unto them save it were by the Holy Ghost.
> But behold, ye have both heard my voice, and seen me; and ye are my sheep, and ye are numbered among those whom the Father hath given me. (3 Nephi 15:21–24)

Jesus went on to instruct the Nephite Twelve about other peoples in other places, stating

> And verily, verily, I say unto you that I have other sheep, which are not of this land, neither of the land of Jerusalem, neither in any parts of that land round about whither I have been to minister.
> For they of whom I speak are they who have not as yet heard my

voice; neither have I at any time manifested myself unto them.

But I have received a commandment of the Father that I shall go unto them, and that they shall hear my voice, and shall be numbered among my sheep, that there may be one fold and one shepherd; therefore I go to show myself unto them. (3 Nephi 16:1–3)

Concerning these other people, President Joseph Fielding Smith offered an interesting view: "When the Savior taught the Nephites he informed them that he had 'other sheep' which were not of the Nephites, neither of the land of Jerusalem, and these also were to hear his voice and be ministered to by him. It is reasonable for us to conclude that among these others who were hidden from the rest of the world, he likewise chose disciples—perhaps twelve—to perform like functions and minister unto their people with the same fulness of divine authority." [10]

Jesus concluded the first day of his visit to Joseph's remnant in the Western Hemisphere by providing those sacred experiences involving the little children and their families, which we have already discussed (see 3 Nephi 17 and chapter 3 herein). He also gave instructions on the administration of the sacrament and the importance of prayer (3 Nephi 18). But just before he left the multitude for the night, he called together the Twelve and gave them additional power through the laying on of hands (Moroni 2:2). The Fifth Gospel states:

And now I go unto the Father, because it is expedient that I should go unto the Father for your sakes.

And it came to pass that when Jesus had made an end of these sayings, he touched with his hand the disciples whom he had chosen, one by one, even until he had touched them all, and spake unto them as he touched them.

And the multitude heard not the words which he spake, therefore they did not bear record; but the disciples bare record that he gave them power to give the Holy Ghost. And I will show unto you hereafter that this record is true.

And it came to pass that when Jesus had touched them all, there came a cloud and overshadowed the multitude that they could not see Jesus.

And while they were overshadowed he departed from them, and ascended into heaven. And the disciples saw and did bear record that he ascended again into heaven. (3 Nephi 18:35–39)

Jesus did not tell the people specifically why he was returning to his Father in Heaven after the first day—only that it was for their sakes (verse 35) and that he had to fulfill other commandments the Father had given him (3 Nephi 18:27). Perhaps he wanted to allow people time to digest what had just transpired, report to his Father, and visit other peoples. Earlier, Jesus had said that he had "received a commandment of the Father" that he should go to these other sheep, "that they shall hear [his] voice, and shall be numbered among [his] sheep, that there may be one fold and one shepherd" (3 Nephi 16:3). What we do know is that on that first day, as a result of the fulfillment of the old order, or law of Moses, the Savior began to personally put into operation the organization of the new order—his Church—with all the gifts and powers that were required to lead families to perfection. By the time he ascended into heaven at the end of the three-day period, he had conferred every power upon the Twelve that they needed to direct the Church. Though the multitude did not hear what Jesus said to the Twelve just before he left at the end of the first day, his words to them were preserved by Moroni:

> The words of Christ, which he spake unto his disciples, the twelve whom he had chosen, as he laid his hands upon them—
> And he called them by name, saying: Ye shall call on the Father in my name, in mighty prayer; and after ye have done this ye shall have power that to him upon whom ye shall lay your hands, ye shall give the Holy Ghost; and in my name shall ye give it, for thus do mine apostles.
> Now Christ spake these words unto them at the time of his first appearing; and the multitude heard it not, but the disciples heard it; and on as many as they laid their hands, fell the Holy Ghost. (Moroni 2:1–3)

TRANSLATED BEINGS

Near the end of his three-day sojourn among the remnant of Joseph in the Western Hemisphere, Jesus called the Twelve Apostles together and interviewed them one by one. Most of their training was complete—at least that part that Jesus had been commissioned to deliver personally. He asked each of them a question: "What is it that ye desire of me, after that I am gone to the Father?" (3 Nephi 28:1). Good teachers want and need to know what effect their teaching has had on their pupils. Here we see Jesus inviting personal, intimate feedback.

Perhaps the defining characteristic of the Savior's ministry was his desire and ability to teach "one by one." For example, after he appeared to the multitude at the Bountiful temple he invited the twenty-five hundred individuals to come forward "one by one" and feel the wounds in his hands and feet and side (3 Nephi 11:14–15). In that most moving of stories in scripture, he blessed the little children "one by one" (3 Nephi 17). And now, at the end of his three-day ministry, he interviewed, tutored, and touched his Twelve Apostles "one by one"—a fitting conclusion to his many examples of perfect pedagogy.

In response to his question and his solicitous concern for their feelings and desires, nine of the Twelve asked to come "speedily" into the Savior's presence in his kingdom (3 Nephi 28:2). Jesus granted their request, promising that they would find rest (3 Nephi 28:3). Throughout the scriptures, we find the term *rest* being used in a significant and special way. According to the Lord, rest means "the fulness of his [God's] glory" (D&C 84:24). On this occasion with the twelve American Apostles, Jesus essentially promised nine of them exaltation after their mortal ministries were finished.

However, three of the Twelve had a different wish, which they apparently felt ashamed to express (3 Nephi 28:5). But Jesus knew their thoughts and said, "ye have desired the thing which John, my beloved, who was with me in my ministry, before I was lifted up by the Jews, desired of me. Therefore, more blessed are ye, for ye shall never taste of death; but ye shall live to behold all the doings of the Father unto the children of men, even until all things shall be fulfilled according to the will of the Father, when I shall come in my glory with the powers of heaven" (3 Nephi 28:6–7). Both John the Beloved and these three Nephites were to become translated beings, to remain on earth until the time of their resurrection (compare John 21:20–24). Jesus went on to explain the nature and status of translated beings to his American Apostles (3 Nephi 28:8–10).

1. They would never endure the pains of death.
2. They would be changed from a translated condition to a resurrected condition "in the twinkling of an eye" at the time of the glorious second coming of Christ.
3. They would not experience the pains and frailties of the mortal body.
4. They would not experience sorrow, except for the sins of humankind.
5. They would continue their work to help bring souls unto Christ.
6. They would have a fulness of joy and become as the Father and the Son.

The Prophet Joseph Smith spoke about the "doctrine of translation" and its relationship to the priesthood. He said,

> Now the doctrine of translation is a power which belongs to this Priesthood. There are many things which belong to the powers of the Priesthood and the keys thereof, that have been kept hid from before the foundation of the world; they are hid from the wise and prudent to be revealed in the last times.
>
> Many have supposed that the doctrine of translation was a doctrine whereby men were taken immediately into the presence of God, and into an eternal fullness, but this is a mistaken idea. Their place of habitation is that of the terrestrial order, and a place prepared for such characters He held in reserve to be ministering angels unto many planets, and who as yet have not entered into so great a fullness as those who are resurrected from the dead . . .
>
> This distinction is made between the doctrine of the actual resurrection and translation: translation obtains deliverance from the tortures and sufferings of the body, but their existence will prolong as to the labors and toils of the ministry, before they can enter into so great a rest and glory.[11]

Regarding translated beings, especially the Three Nephites, the following summary is instructive:

> In the overall scheme of things, and under the divine superintendence of our God, who knows perfectly well when and under what circumstances to send his servants to earth, the Lord occasionally has chosen to translate his servants. That is, he has caused a change to come upon their bodies such that they are "sanctified in the flesh," no longer subject to sin, pain, bodily decay, and death, but are not resurrected (3 Nephi 28:7–9, 39) . . .
>
> Translated beings are still mortal, but their bodies have been transformed from a telestial to a terrestrial order. . . . They are given great power and are able to appear and disappear as they choose (3 Nephi 28:27–30). The nature of their activities is determined and governed by the Lord, and only he knows their whereabouts. . . . They remain in this condition until the second coming of Christ in glory, at which time they will undergo a change equivalent to death, being changed from mortality to resurrected and glorified immortality (3 Nephi 28:7–8, 39–40) . . .
>
> Persons in scripture who have been translated include Enoch and his city (Genesis 5:21–24; D&C 107:48–49; Moses 7:68–69), Melchizedek and the city of Salem (Alma 13:14–19; JST, Genesis

14:25–40), Moses (Alma 45:19), Elijah (2 Kings 2; D&C 110:13), Alma the Younger (Alma 45:18–19), Nephi the son of Helaman (3 Nephi 1:2–3; 2:9), John the Beloved (John 21:20–23; D&C 7), and the Three Nephite apostles (3 Nephi 28).[12]

In a final gesture of love and blessing, Jesus "touched with his finger" nine of the Twelve and then departed. The three who were to be translated "were caught up into heaven, and saw and heard unspeakable things" (3 Nephi 28:13; compare verse 36). "And whether they were in the body or out of the body, they could not tell; for it did seem unto them like a transfiguration of them, that they were changed from this body of flesh into an immortal state, that they could behold the things of God" (3 Nephi 28:15).

Translation, like transfiguration, is a matter of physics. The physical bodies of translated beings are changed to a higher state of existence to be able to enjoy the presence of divine beings, and in order to help mortals progress toward perfection and eternal life.

CONCLUSION

Though Christ would leave his American disciples at the end of three days, the Church organization he established, as well as the doctrines, ordinances, and covenants he taught, remained. He had called and ordained twelve other Apostles in the New World to minister unto the people. "Their call was to give complete devotion to their spiritual ministry and to trust in God's—and the people's—providence for their temporal needs." [13] They were to serve the people with unswerving dedication. But they were always to take their direction, their cues, if you will, from Deity.

Perhaps that is why on the morning of the second day of Jesus's visit to the Western Hemisphere, before he had appeared again, we find the Twelve engaged in prayer. And of all the things they could have prayed for, it was the Holy Ghost they desired most. As recorded,

And the twelve did teach the multitude; and behold, they did cause that the multitude should kneel down upon the face of the earth, and should pray unto the Father in the name of Jesus.

And the disciples did pray unto the Father also in the name of Jesus. And it came to pass that they arose and ministered unto the people.

And when they had ministered those same words which Jesus had spoken—nothing varying from the words which Jesus had spoken—behold, they knelt again and prayed to the Father in the name of Jesus.

And they did pray for that which they most desired; and they desired that the Holy Ghost should be given unto them (3 Nephi 19:6–9).

The Twelve Apostles were commissioned to teach and lead the Church in ancient America, but always under the direction of Jesus Christ. In fact, the Twelve had been given a perfect object lesson on how the Church was to operate when the Savior taught them about the sacrament.

And it came to pass that Jesus commanded his disciples that they should bring forth some bread and wine unto him.

And while they were gone for bread and wine, he commanded the multitude that they should sit themselves down upon the earth.

And when the disciples had come with bread and wine, he took of the bread and brake and blessed it; and he gave unto the disciples and commanded that they should eat.

And when they had eaten and were filled, he commanded that they should give unto the multitude. (3 Nephi 18:1–4)

The Savior ministered to and instructed the Twelve. They in turn ministered to and instructed the other members of Christ's Church—all for the purpose of helping the people to establish Zion. As 4 Nephi tells us, this was how the Church functioned for some sixteen decades and how the people were blessed immeasurably because of it.

NOTES

1. Bruce R. McConkie, "The Purifying Power of Gethsemane," *Ensign*, May 1985, 11.

2. Joseph Smith, *History of the Church of Jesus Christ of Latter-day Saints* (Salt Lake City: Deseret Book, 1978), 4:538.

3. Joseph Fielding Smith, *Answers to Gospel Questions* (Salt Lake City: Deseret Book, 1957), 122.

4. Ibid.

5. Joseph Smith, *Teachings of the Prophet Joseph Smith*, sel. Joseph Fielding Smith (Salt Lake City: Deseret Book, 1977), 181.

6. Smith, *Answers to Gospel Questions*, 126.

7. Thomas S. Monson, "Be of Good Cheer," *Ensign*, May 2009, 92.

8. *Journal of Discourses*, 26 vols. (London: Latter-day Saints' Book Depot, 1854–86), 18:167–168.

9. Talmage, *Jesus the Christ* (Salt Lake City: Deseret Book, 1962), 728–729.

10. Smith, *Answers to Gospel Questions*, 122.

11. *Teachings of the Prophet Joseph Smith,* 170–71.

12. Robert L. Millet, et al., *LDS Beliefs: A Doctrinal Reference* (Salt Lake City: Deseret Book, 2011), 637–638.

13. Jeffrey R. Holland, *Christ and the New Covenant* (Salt Lake City: Deseret Book, 1997), 264–265.

6

The Pure Gospel Defined

ON THE THIRD DAY OF HIS VISIT TO THE NEW WORLD, JESUS DELIV-ered a unique discourse to the twelve disciples. A characteristic of the New Testament Gospels is their report of Jesus's prominent sermons. As the Fifth Gospel, 3 Nephi also contains discourses of the Savior and, in this instance, his unmatched discourse on what the gospel really is. In it he personally defined the nature and importance of "his Gospel" and taught the Twelve Apostles in the New World how all things center on the Atonement. In the Church, we speak much about the gospel of Jesus Christ, and we rightly point out that the Book of Mormon contains the fulness of that Gospel (D&C 20:9; 27:5; 42:12). We frequently discuss what the Lord meant by that declaration, including how the term *gospel* should be defined. But it has been my observation that far too infrequently do we first look to the meaning given by the very Being whose gospel it is—Jesus Christ. This definition and the discourse in which it was discussed are found in 3 Nephi 27, a chapter that compels us to view 3 Nephi as the Fifth Gospel.

Nowhere else in sacred writ outside of 3 Nephi 27 does Jesus personally define the term *gospel* with such power and clarity. Nowhere else in all of scripture does he proclaim personal authorship (and ownership) of the gospel he preached nor explain it in such exquisite simplicity as the carrying out of his Father's will. Nowhere else in scripture does he connect so directly and succinctly his Father's will with the Crucifixion,

Resurrection, and Final Judgment and then link them so concretely to the universal salvation he has offered to all humankind. Third Nephi 27 stands at the doctrinal apex of Jesus's post-Resurrection visit to the New World. It is the culminating discourse of his New World teachings on the nature of salvation.

SETTING

The setting for this capstone instruction was Jesus's appearance to his disciples on the last day of his sojourn among them. They were "united in mighty prayer and fasting" after traveling and teaching the things they had previously seen and heard (3 Nephi 27:1). Jesus showed himself unto them as a direct response to their devotional activity (verse 2). This reminds us of other Book of Mormon examples of the stunning results that come from mighty prayer. Nephi (see 1 Nephi 18:3), Enos (see Enos 1:4), Alma (see Alma 8:10), the Sons of Mosiah (see Alma 17:3–4), and Nephi, son of Nephi (see 3 Nephi 1:11–12), are only a few of the many other witnesses that affirm the validity of this spiritual law. Mighty prayer is a conduit of power. It opens the gates of heaven.

The spiritual power generated by these disciples derived from their unity of purpose and united actions. They were following the precepts and example of their Master, especially his repeated call for unity among them. They sought an answer to the question about what the name of the Church should be. Jesus not only answered their specific query but also laid the foundation for the watershed discourse and spiritual feast that they were about to receive on a topic central to the plan of salvation. He taught them the proper, authorized name of his church—the Church of Jesus Christ, that it would be built upon *his* Gospel (3 Nephi 27:9), and that it would display the works of the Father, which he would "show forth . . . in it" (verse 10).

"MY GOSPEL"

After testifying that his Church was founded on his Gospel, the Savior provided some descriptions of the term so there would be no misunderstandings:

> Behold I have given unto you my gospel, and this is the gospel which I have given unto you—that I came into the world to do the

will of my Father, because my Father sent me.

And my Father sent me that I might be lifted up upon the cross; and after that I had been lifted up upon the cross, that I might draw all men unto me, that as I have been lifted up by men even so should men be lifted up by the Father, to stand before me, to be judged of their works, whether they be good or whether they be evil—

And for this cause have I been lifted up; therefore, according to the power of the Father I will draw all men unto me, that they may be judged according to their works.

And it shall come to pass, that whoso repenteth and is baptized in my name shall be filled; and if he endureth to the end, behold, him will I hold guiltless before my Father at that day when I shall stand to judge the world. (3 Nephi 27:13–16)

These verses constitute a singular and stunning discourse on the nature of the gospel delivered by the very source of good news himself. The English word *gospel* literally means "good news." It "is derived from the Old English *gódspel*, a combination of *gód* (good) and *spel* or *spiel* (news, tidings) . . . [which is] a proper translation of the Latin transliteration (*evangelium*) of the original term *euangelion*, 'good news.'"[1] This accords well with the meaning found in latter-day revelation: "glad tidings" (D&C 76:40), even "glad tidings of great joy" (D&C 79:1).

This surely is the sense in which Jesus used the word with his American Israelites. For what better or more supernal news could have been delivered to them than the Great Creator himself came down to the earth to be lifted up upon the Cross as a redemptive offering so all humankind could be lifted up in a resurrected state, overcoming physical death, with the opportunity to overcome spiritual death and be declared guiltless?

One of the greatest contributions of 3 Nephi to our understanding of Jesus's mortal ministry is so simple as to be almost overlooked, namely, its confirmation that Jesus knew and used the term *gospel*, as a noun, in his preaching, teaching, and exhortation. Though the Greek noun *euangelion* (from which our English *gospel* derives) is found in the New Testament Gospel accounts,[2] some scholars believe it "improbable that Jesus himself should have used the [Greek] noun or its Semitic equivalent,"[3] which is *basorah*. Rather, many authorities attribute the first use of the term *gospel* to the Apostle Paul.[4] Certainly, Paul spoke often of the message of salvation as "good tidings." He used the noun *euangelion* some sixty times in his writings—in every one of his letters. But the fact remains that the Synoptic Gospels—Matthew, Mark, and Luke—attribute to Jesus the first use of the term *euangelion*, "glad tidings" or "gospel." Thus, 3 Nephi supports and verifies the New Testament Gospels and helps us appreciate why those ancient writers should be taken at face value over the arguments of modern skeptics.

Even more important than confirming Jesus's knowledge and use of the term *gospel*, 3 Nephi reports that Jesus declared unequivocally that *he* was (and is) the author of the good news or glad tidings of true and lasting salvation. It is "my gospel," he says, and this serves to stand as a stark differentiation between his glad tidings and other messages of "good news" in the ancient world.

We know that other "good or glad tidings" circulated during the period roughly contemporaneous with Jesus's mortal existence. For instance, a Priene calendar inscription dated to around 9 BC speaks of the birth of the divine emperor Caesar Augustus (emperor during the first fourteen years of Jesus's mortal existence) as "the beginning of good tidings" to the world.[5] In this regard, it is interesting to compare how Mark introduces his Gospel account: "The beginning of the gospel [good tidings] of Jesus Christ, the Son of God" (Mark 1:1). Mark notifies readers that the good tidings he is reporting are different from any other good news that others might celebrate, including (and especially) reports of the coming of a perceived divine ruler such as Caesar Augustus. The fact that Mark appeals immediately (Mark 1:2–3) to Old Testament messianic prophecies to lay the foundation for his discussion indicates a desire on his part that readers understand from the start the profound and eternal significance of the true "gospel," as opposed to, say, political "good news." For, "As it is written in the prophets, Behold I send my messenger before thy face, which shall prepare thy way before thee. The voice of one crying in the wilderness, Prepare ye the way of the Lord, make his paths straight."

By declaring the gospel he had taught to his New World disciples to be *his* Gospel, he essentially certified its divine origins and effective power. When Jesus appeared, everyone knew he was the true Messiah and Son of God. His very appearance to them those three days in the land Bountiful was proof of that. The miracles that he performed and the force of his presence were evidence of his divinity. By declaring that the gospel he preached was *his* Gospel, the glad tidings of the true and living Messiah, Jesus was testifying that only his teachings were divine, that only they had power to save and exalt. What better way could there be to teach His disciples that they must not deviate from his prescribed course.

The Apostle Paul would similarly warn disciples in the Old World that only Christ's own Gospel, only the teachings that originated with him, were valid even though others, including angels, might present a different gospel. Said he,

> But though we, or an angel from heaven, preach any other gospel unto you than that which we have preached unto you, let him be accursed . . .
>
> But I certify you, brethren, that the gospel which was preached of me is not after man.
>
> For I neither received it of man, neither was I taught it, but by the revelation of Jesus Christ. (Galatians 1:8, 11–12)

Thus, Paul's warning to the Galatians parallels Jesus own declaration to the Nephites. It is *his* Gospel that saves and none other!

Origin of the Use of the Term "Good News"

The New Testament writers' use of the term "glad tidings," or "good news," and certainly Jesus's use of it, cannot be thought to have derived from their familiarity with Greek literature. Most of them were not scholars of classical writings. Rather, it seems to be Jesus's quotation of Isaiah where we find the source for the earliest Christian use and understanding of the term *gospel*. This is not startling given our Lord's preference for Isaiah as seen in both the New Testament and the Book of Mormon, wherein we find many direct quotations of the great eighth-century-BC prophet. We are struck especially by Jesus's unequivocal endorsement of Isaiah reported in 3 Nephi 23.

A pivotal episode in helping us to understand the early Christian use of the term gospel as "glad tidings/good news," and particularly the disciples' amazing and immediate grasp of its significance, is found in Luke's report of Jesus's visit to the Nazareth synagogue early in his ministry.

> And he came to Nazareth, where he had been brought up: and, as his custom was, he went into the synagogue on the sabbath day, and stood up for to read.
>
> And there was delivered unto him the book of the prophet Esaias. And when he had opened the book, he found the place where it was written,

The Spirit of the Lord is upon me, because he hath anointed me to preach the gospel to the poor; he hath sent me to heal the brokenhearted, to preach deliverance to the captives, and recovering of sight to the blind, to set at liberty them that are bruised,

To preach the acceptable year of the Lord.

And he closed the book, and he gave it again to the minister, and sat down. And the eyes of all them that were in the synagogue were fastened on him.

And he began to say unto them, This day is this scripture fulfilled in your ears. (Luke 4:16–21)

Many of the disciples, if not all, were acquainted with Isaiah 61:1–2 and recognized it to be a powerful messianic prophecy. Jesus was its fulfillment and the One who would "preach the *gospel*" (emphasis added) in a day of triumph. In addition, there were other passages from Isaiah, well-known in Jesus's day, that refer to a coming deliverance of God's people, a messianic triumph and glorious future for Zion, and that used the term "glad tidings" (see Isaiah 40:9, 52:7). These passages educated and prepared some Jews to expect a fulfillment of the prophesied "glad tidings" of redemption and deliverance in the form of a man. Thus, when Jesus quoted passages from Isaiah that used the term *gospel*, no great explanatory discourse was needed. Followers believed he was the Deliverer. What eventually proved to be surprising to the disciples was that the "glad tidings" of deliverance and redemption came not by way of military might or governmental power, but through the ignominious death of the very One who preached the glad tidings of deliverance.   .

THE FATHER'S WILL

After Jesus proclaimed personal authorship of the gospel he had been teaching the Nephites, he described the essence of "the Gospel" as his carrying out the will of his Father. "This is the gospel which I have given unto you," he said, "that I came into the world to do the will of my Father, because my Father sent me" (3 Nephi 27:13). By carrying out his Father's will, he acted as his Father's agent, seeking only to satisfy his Father's desire, design, intention, and plan. He had said so earlier during his mortal ministry, "I seek not mine own will, but the will of the Father which hath sent me" (John 5:30).

The constant and consistent picture presented by the scriptures from beginning to end is of Jesus Christ, the Only Begotten Son, seeking only to carry out the will of his Father.

- In a grand council, held before the world came into being, the pre-mortal Jesus offered to become the executor of the Father's plan, "even the messenger of salvation" (D&C 93:8). On that occasion, he said, "Father, thy will be done, and the glory be thine forever" (Moses 4:2).

- During his earthly mission, in the Garden of Gethsemane, Jesus's plea was to have the bitter cup removed if possible, "nevertheless, not what I will, but what thou wilt" (Mark 14:36). Even as the intensity of Gethsemane's torturous experience became acute, his prayer was the same, "O my Father, if this cup may not pass away from me, except I drink it, thy will be done. . . . and [he] prayed the third time, saying the same words" (Matthew 26:42, 44; see also Luke 22:42).

- During the last moments of his life, and literally with his dying breath, Jesus proclaimed his fulfillment of the promise made in the pre-mortal council of heaven. "Jesus, when he had cried again with a loud voice, saying, Father, it is finished, thy will is done, yielded up the ghost" (JST, Matthew 27:50).

- As already noted, when Jesus first appeared to the people in America, of all the ways he could have introduced himself, he chose to declare his obedience to the Father's will: "And it came to pass that he stretched forth his hand and spake unto the people, saying: Behold, I am Jesus Christ, whom the prophets testified shall come into the world. And behold, I am the light and the life of the world; and I have drunk out of that bitter cup which the Father hath given me, and have glorified the Father in taking upon me the sins of the world, in the which *I have suffered the will of the Father in all things from the beginning*" (3 Nephi 11:9–11; emphasis added).

- In a powerful and atonement-centered revelation to the Prophet Joseph Smith in March 1830, the Savior again proclaimed his identity by reference to the Father's will: "I am Jesus Christ; I came by the will of the Father; and I do his will" (D&C 19:24).

The scriptural record is impressive; every thought and action of Jesus Christ was centered on his commitment to fulfill the will of his Father. We have been told that this too must be the quest of every true disciple of the Son of God, that our allegiance must go beyond lip service to Deity, that we, like Jesus, must focus on the Father's will. Because of 3 Nephi we know that there is no question that the gospel of Jesus Christ consists of one fundamental, overriding principle: doing the will of our Father in Heaven, subordinating our will to his, having our desires "being swallowed up in the will of the Father" as exemplified by Jesus (Mosiah 15:7). Furthermore, because of 3 Nephi we also know that the tangible expression of honoring the Father's will consists of fully embracing the plan of salvation, and participating in its ordinances. This is what Jesus called the doctrine of Christ (3 Nephi 11:31–40). Elder Bruce R. McConkie explained it this way:

> Salvation does not come to those who merely confess Christ with their lips, or even to those who go about doing good works (as men generally view good works). It is reserved for those who do the very things which constitute the will of the Father, namely: (1) Accept and believe the true gospel, thus gaining faith in Christ, and thus believing in the prophets sent by Christ to reveal his truths, Joseph Smith being the greatest of these in this dispensation; (2) Repent; (3) Be baptized by a legal administrator who has power from God to bind on earth and seal in heaven; (4) Receive the gift of the Holy Ghost, also by the authorized act of a duly appointed priesthood bearer; and (5) Endure in righteousness and devotion to the truth, keeping every standard of personal righteousness that appertains to the gospel, until the end of one's mortal probation.[6]

THE CROSS

The Gospel or "good news" in its most basic and pared-down description, then, consists of the Son fulfilling the will of the Father. Jesus told his twelve disciples that the will of the Father ultimately centered on the Cross: "I came into the world to do the will of the Father, because my Father sent me. And my Father sent me that I might be lifted up upon the cross" (3 Nephi 27:13–14). For Jesus, as well as his prophet-witnesses in the Book of Mormon, the focus of his ministry came to rest on his being lifted up upon the cruel Cross of crucifixion. Some six hundred years beforehand, Nephi saw in vision that the Messiah "was lifted up upon the cross and slain for the sins of the world" (1 Nephi 11:33). Even before that, the brother of Jared was told to "write the things which he had seen" but that "they were forbidden to come unto the children of men until after that [the Lord] should be lifted up upon the cross" (Ether 4:1). And the great prophet Jacob desired "that all men would believe in Christ, and view his death, and suffer his cross" (Jacob 1:8).

It seems ironic that one of the most distinctive teachings others see in LDS theology about the Atonement is a perceived emphasis we put on Gethsemane as a place of redemptive suffering. And yet a central idea of the Book of Mormon (the keystone of our religion) is clearly grounded in the importance of the Cross. But that doesn't seem to receive much "press" or is misunderstood. One of my colleagues tells the story about a woman who asked a Protestant pastor how he could associate with Mormons, seeing how they "don't even believe that Jesus died on the cross." When pressed by the Pastor as to where she thought Latter-day Saints believed Jesus died, she responded, "Oh, I don't mean that, I mean, they don't believe he died for our sins on the cross."[7]

Third Nephi starkly and powerfully corrects such errant notions about LDS theology. The Savior clearly emphasized the singular importance of the Cross. Because we adore and worship Jesus Christ as the King of Kings and Lord of Lords, we cherish the image, symbol, and metaphor that is the Cross. This does not, in any way, diminish the importance of Gethsemane. We must never abandon or even treat lightly our knowledge of Gethsemane as a place of redemptive suffering. But, on the other hand, we must never diminish the monumental importance of the Cross. Thankfully its significance is recapitulated in the unforgettable narrative of 3 Nephi 27.

Both Gethsemane and the Cross constitute the awful, terrible suffering and sacrifice that was the Atonement. Elder B. H. Roberts instructively put it this way: "If it be true, and it is, that men value things in proportion to what they cost, then how dear to them must be the Atonement, since it cost Christ so much in suffering that he may be said to have been baptized by blood-sweat in Gethsemane, before he reached the climax of his passion, on Calvary."[8] On the Cross, "all the infinite agonies and merciless pains of Gethsemane recurred."[9] Perhaps, the Savior chose to emphasize the Cross during his New World discourse because it represents the climax of his passion, his suffering. As President Gordon B. Hinckley said, "He worked out [redemption] in the Garden of Gethsemane and upon the cross of Calvary which made His gift immortal, universal, and everlasting."[10]

The Cross is one of those universal symbols of God's love and salvation that we share and reverence along with the rest of the Christian world. We rejoice in the Cross for what it represents—not because we are worried about what other Christians may say or think about us, but because passages like 3 Nephi tell us how our risen Lord felt about the Cross and how important it was and is in the Father's great plan of happiness (see 3 Nephi 11, 12, 27). On occasion we do find expressions from other Christians that are so eloquent we want to make them our own. A. W. Tozer penned such a sentiment, one that actually summarizes teachings from the Book of Mormon and other restoration scripture. He wrote,

> The cross is the most revolutionary thing ever to appear among men.
>
> The cross of Roman times knew no compromise; it never made concessions. It won all its arguments by killing its opponent and silencing him for good. It spared not Christ, but slew Him the same as the rest. He was alive when they hung Him on that cross and completely dead when they took Him down six hours later. That was the cross the first time it appeared in Christian history . . .
>
> The cross effects its ends by destroying one established pattern, the victim's, and creating another pattern, its own. Thus it always has its way. It wins by defeating its opponent and imposing its will upon him. It always dominates. It never compromises, never dickers nor confers, never surrenders a point for the sake of peace. It cares not for peace; it cares only to end its opposition as fast as possible.
>
> With perfect knowledge of all this, Christ said, "If any man will come after me, let him deny himself, and take up his cross, and follow me." So the cross not only brings Christ's life to an end, it ends also the first life, the old life, of every one of His true followers. It destroys the old pattern, the Adam pattern, in the believer's life, and brings it to an end. Then the God who raised Christ from the dead raises the believer and a new life begins.
>
> This, and nothing less, is true Christianity . . .
>
> We must do something about the cross, and one of two things only we can do—flee it or die upon it.[11]

And so it comes down to this when considering the meaning of the Cross for us personally. We can either ignore it or we can embrace it and die upon it—meaning we can be transformed, we can crucify the natural man, we can yield to the enticings of the Holy Spirit. The crucifixion wounds that identify Jesus can become the wounds that identify us as committed disciples. The Apostle Paul put it this way: "And they that are Christ's have crucified the flesh with the affections and lusts" (Galatians 5:24). This was Paul's personal experience for he stated, "I am crucified with Christ: nevertheless I live; yet not I, but Christ liveth in me: and the life which I now live in the flesh I live by the faith of the Son of God, who loved me, and gave himself for me" (Galatians 2:20).

Discipleship is based on identity. The Twelve Apostles in the New World came to know that. It is instructive that immediately after his Resurrection, the wounds Jesus received on the Cross became the identifying marks of his messianic conquest. Luke records the episode of Jesus's appearance to certain disciples on the road to Emmaus. He appeared to them and spent some time with them. But they did not recognize him *until* "he took bread, and blessed it, and brake, and gave to them. And their eyes were opened, and [then] they knew him" (Luke 24:30–31). Undoubtedly, recognition came when they finally saw the wounds in his hands and wrists! Discipleship is predicated on identity.

Significantly, Jesus will also identify himself to the Jewish people as the once crucified but now risen Messiah by means of those wounds, those sure signs or tokens left by the nails of the Cross. "And then shall the Jews look upon me and say: What are these wounds in thine hands and in thy feet? Then shall they know that I am the Lord; for I will say unto them: These wounds are the wounds with which I was wounded in the house of my friends. I am he who was lifted up. I am Jesus that was crucified. I am the Son of God. And then shall they weep because of their iniquities; then shall they lament because they persecuted their king" (D&C 45:51–53).

LIFTED UP

Just as the Cross, or rather what happened on the Cross, can transform us, it can lift us and comfort us in times of sadness and tragedy. Contemplation of what happened on the Cross can help us cope when things get bad. In a moving comment, Richard Mouw gave this insight:

> We admit we can't understand the mysteries of God's purposes. But we can go to the cross of Jesus Christ. We can see that, at the Cross, God took upon himself abandonment, abuse, forlornness, depth of suffering. Christ himself cried out from the depths of his being, 'My God, why hast thou forsaken me?' When we see what God did through Jesus Christ we can say, 'There is a safe place in the universe, in the shelter of the Almighty, in the shadow of the Most High.' That place is Calvary.[12]

Knowing that God himself suffered unjustly and infinitely helps us bear our afflictions with greater patience and faith, giving us hope that we can be exalted because of the things that we suffer (see Hebrews 5:8–9). Making Jesus's example of suffering on the Cross our model can help us to "submit to all things which the Lord seeth fit to inflict upon [us]" (Mosiah 3:19). Elder Jeffrey R. Holland observed that, although we may not understand why certain things happen as they do, obedience and submission to God (whether physically or spiritually) to the very end of our lives "are the key to our blessings and our salvation. In the suffering as well as in the serving, we must be willing to be like our Savior." [13]

As Professor Mouw intimates, in times of sorrow and suffering, the Savior's own unparalleled suffering, in effect, draws all serious truth-seekers to him. But it also draws to him all mortals who seriously contemplate their awful, sinful state. The power of the Atonement will draw all men and women to the Savior because his sacrifice, culminating on the Cross, is the only way we can escape the ravages of this fallen world. That is really what the atoning sacrifice of Christ is—a remedy to the Fall, a way, the *only* way in fact, to fix that which is broken, a way to restore wholeness. And that is what I believe Jesus is trying to teach all of us when he stated to his disciples in the New World, "I had been lifted up upon the cross, that I might draw all men unto me" (3 Nephi 27:14). Writing on the nature of man's mortal, fallen condition, Blaise Pascal, seventeenth-century French mathematician and philosopher, said: "The Incarnation shows man the greatness of his misery by the greatness of the remedy which he required." [14]

Only the Atonement, capsulized by Jesus in the visual image of him being "lifted up upon the cross" (3 Nephi 27:14), can lift *us* and exalt *us*, can redeem *us* from the ravages of this mortal fallen world. Jesus also taught this doctrine during the last week of his mortal life using much of the same language found in 3 Nephi 27. After the voice of the Father was heard testifying of the Son, "Jesus answered and said, This voice came not because of me, but for your sakes. Now is the judgment of this world: now shall the prince of this world be cast out. And I, if I be lifted up from the earth, will draw all men unto me. This he said, signifying what death he should die" (John 12:30–33).

That Jesus repeated this instruction to his American disciples highlights its tremendous importance. Furthermore, in the New World Jesus used impressive rhetorical parallelism to emphasize the universal resurrection of all humankind and a subsequent universal Judgment made possible by his sacrifice. He stated that just as he had "been lifted up by men," even so all men would "be lifted up by the Father, to stand before [him], to be judged of their works" (3 Nephi 27:14). In my view, the verse that follows it is not simply a restatement of Jesus's sacrifice, but a verification of the role and power of God the Father in bringing to pass all his purposes, including the Resurrection and Final Judgment. "And for this cause have I been lifted up; therefore, according to the power of the Father I will draw all men unto me, that they may be judged according to their works" (verse 15).

The great power of God the Father is the power to give life (John 5:21, 26) and ultimately the power to raise up his children to the same condition he enjoys, a glorified state of eternal existence (Moses 1:39). During his earthly ministry Jesus taught of his Father's life-giving power and how it extended to the Son: "For as the Father raiseth up the dead, and quickeneth them; even so the Son quickeneth whom he will. . . . For as the Father hath life in himself; so hath he given to the Son to have life in himself" (John 5: 21, 26). And because the Son had "life in himself" every other mortal may have life eternally if they repent, are baptized in the name of Jesus Christ, and try to live as Jesus Christ lived. That is essentially the message with which Jesus concluded his unique, Gospel-defining discourse:

> Now this is the commandment: Repent, all ye ends of the earth, and come unto me and be baptized in my name, that ye may be sanctified by the reception of the Holy Ghost, that ye may stand spotless before me at the last day. Verily, verily, I say unto you, this is my gospel; and ye know the things that ye must do in my church; for the works which ye have seen me do that shall ye also do; for that which ye have seen me do even that shall ye do. (3 Nephi 27: 20–21)

CONCLUSION

The Gospel or good news, as Jesus Christ described it in this powerful, unparalleled discourse given to the Twelve in the Western Hemisphere, was presented in fairly simple terms. But its ramifications are quite complex. The Son of God, who is also God himself, condescended to come to earth to do the will of his Father. The Father's will was that his Son be lifted up upon a cross to suffer for the sins of the world so that all humankind, in turn, could be lifted up through the power of the Resurrection and be judged according to their works. All of this constitutes the Atonement of Jesus Christ. In commentary that is both elevating and instructive, Elder Bruce R. McConkie stated:

> Viewed from our mortal position, the gospel is all that is required to take us back to the Eternal Presence, there to be crowned with glory and honor, immortality and eternal life. To gain these greatest of all rewards, two things are required. The first is the atonement by which all men are raised in immortality, with those who believe and obey ascending also unto eternal life. This atoning sacrifice was the work of our Blessed Lord, and he has done his work. The second requisite is obedience on our part to the laws and ordinances of the gospel. Thus *the gospel is, in effect, the atonement.*[15]

Perhaps no other text now known helps us connect the concepts "gospel" and "atonement" in such a clear and distinctive way as 3 Nephi, the Fifth Gospel. From one of the other Gospels we know that "the Gospel" existed in the beginning. According to the Joseph Smith Translation of the Bible, "In the beginning was the gospel preached through the Son. And the gospel was the word, and the word was with the Son, and the Son was with God, and the Son was of God" (JST, John 1:1). We also know that the Atonement existed in the beginning. It was the core, the essence, of the Father's plan of exaltation, established by him in our premortal sojourn (see Moses 1:1–4; Abraham 3:22–28). Consequently, we have come to understand that from creation's dawn through all the ages of eternity nothing ever has, or ever will, equal the Atonement in importance or significance. Through it, all the terms and conditions of the Father's plan were put into operation. Therefore, can we not say as well that nothing ever has or will equal the gospel in importance or significance?

In addition, there is another equivalence we should acknowledge. The King James Version of John 1:1–3 declares that the "word" was also the very person of Jesus Christ, who was in the beginning with the Father and then made flesh on earth to live among mere mortals (John 1:1–3). Thus, the Gospel, the Atonement, and the personage of Jesus Christ are interchangeable expressions of the unparalleled love of God the Father for his children.

This was exactly what Lehi and Nephi learned in their grand vision of eternity six hundred years before the Son of God came to earth. These concepts were distilled for them and encapsulated in the symbol of the Tree of Life:

And he said unto me: Knowest thou the condescension of God? . . . And I looked and beheld the virgin again, bearing a child in her arms. And the angel said unto me: Behold the Lamb of God, yea, even the Son of the Eternal Father! Knowest thou the meaning of the tree which thy father saw? And I answered him, saying: Yea, it is the love of God, which sheddeth itself abroad in the hearts of the children of men; wherefore, it is the most desirable above all things." (1 Nephi 11: 16, 20–22)

Of this vision, Elder Boyd K. Packer stated, "After the people of Lehi left Jerusalem, Lehi had a vision of the Tree of Life. His son Nephi prayed to know its meaning. In answer, he was given a remarkable vision of Christ. . . . That vision is the central message of the Book of Mormon." [16]

So to the other four equivalents we have noted—the Gospel, the Atonement, the Word, and Jesus Christ—we can now add a fifth, the Tree of Life, and we are taken back to the beginning of the Book of Mormon record. Just as the Savior did among the Nephites, it seems we are beginning to be able to expound "all the scriptures in one" (3 Nephi 23:14). The Fifth Gospel is invaluable to our understanding of these matters.

NOTES

1. M. Eugene Boring, "Gospel, Message," in *The New Interpreter's Dictionary of the Bible*, 4 vols. (Nashville: Abingdon, 2006–8), 2:629.

2. The surprising exception is John. He presents no mention of it.

3. O. A. Piper, "Gospel (Message)," in *The Interpreter's Dictionary of the Bible*, 5 vols. (Nashville: Abingdon, 1962), 2:443.

4. Millar Burrows, "The Origin of the Term 'Gospel,'" in *The Journal of Biblical Literature*, vol. 44, no. 1/2 (1925), 22.

5. Ibid., 21.

6. Bruce R. McConkie, *Doctrinal New Testament Commentary*, 3 vols. (Salt Lake City: Bookcraft, 1976), 1:254.

7. Robert L. Millet, *Whatever Happened to the Cross* (Salt Lake City: Deseret Book, 2007), 103.

8. B. H. Roberts, *The Seventy's Course in Theology* (Salt Lake City: Deseret News Press, 1907–12), 4:126.

9. Bruce R. McConkie, Conference Report, April 1985, 10.

10. Gordon B. Hinckley, Christmas Devotional, *Church News*, December 14 1996, 4.

11. A. W. Tozer, *The Root of the Righteousness* (Harrisburg, PA: Christian Publications, 1955), 61–63, cited in John F. MacArthur, *Faith Works*, (Dallas, TX.: Word Publishing, 1993), 205.

12. Richard S. Mouw, "Christian Responses to a World in Crisis," *Fuller Focus*, Spring 2002, 11.

13. Jeffrey R. Holland, *Christ and the New Covenant* (Salt Lake City: Deseret Book, 1997), 304.

14. Blaise Pascal, *Pensees*, part 7, 526. Online resource.

15. Bruce R. McConkie, *A New Witness for the Articles of Faith* (Salt Lake City: Deseret Book, 1985), 134; emphasis added.

16. Boyd K. Packer, Conference Report, April 1986, 75–76.

7

Establishing Zion in the Western Hemisphere

THE LORD HAS ALWAYS WANTED HIS COVENANT PEOPLE TO ESTABLISH Zion in their own day. In this modern dispensation, the Lord's first prophet, Joseph Smith, stated that "we ought to have the building up of Zion as our greatest object."[1] In 1829, even before the Church was organized, the Lord gave this command: "Keep my commandments, and seek to bring forth and establish the cause of Zion" (D&C 6:6; 11:6; 12:6; see also 14:6). There is compelling evidence to show that this was the Lord's desire for the people he visited in the New World and that the people were successful, for a time.

We begin to see this success emerge even before Jesus had completed his three-day sojourn among the people. As the third day dawned, the following was reported:

> And it came to pass that the disciples whom Jesus had chosen began from that time forth to baptize and to teach as many as did come unto them; and as many as were baptized in the name of Jesus were filled with the Holy Ghost.
>
> And many of them saw and heard unspeakable things, which are not lawful to be written.
>
> And they taught, and did minister one to another; and they had all things common among them, every man dealing justly, one with another.

> And it came to pass that they did do all things even as Jesus had commanded them. (3 Nephi 26:17–20)

Most significant is not the visions of unspeakable things that many people experienced, though that is wonderful to contemplate. Rather, the most important thing to see is the results of the Savior's training of the Twelve and the long-term effect that training ultimately had on other people—how the Twelve influenced society. The twelve disciples "began from that time forth to baptize and to teach" (3 Nephi 26:17). And their teaching led to the establishment of the social system sometimes referred to as the united order, which is really the integration of basic components of a Zion society. And, in turn, Zion is really the environment of the celestial kingdom enjoyed in mortality. Moroni says (3 Nephi 26:19) of the people that:

1. they "did minister one to another"
2. "they had all things common among them"
3. "every man [dealt] justly, one with another."

Keeping these characteristics of Nephite society in mind, note how Zion was defined in Enoch's day: "And the Lord called his people Zion, because they were of one heart and one mind, and dwelt in righteousness; and there was no poor among them" (Moses 7:18). Furthermore, the language used to describe the order of the post-Resurrection Church in the Old World is remarkably close to 4 Nephi 1:19. "And all that believed were together, and had all things common" (Acts 2:44). Also, "And the multitude of them that believed were of one heart and of one soul: neither said any of them that ought of the things which he possessed was his own; but they had all things common" (Acts 4:32). The compelling similarity of language and content used to describe Nephite society, the early Church in the Old World, and the city of Enoch of a much earlier time persuades us that all three had established Zion, at least for a time.

Thus we see that attempts to establish Zion began long before the Prophet Joseph Smith's day. The Lord has cared about the establishment of Zion throughout the history of our world. President Marion G. Romney of the First Presidency (1897–1988) taught, "Whenever the Lord has had a people who would accept and live the gospel, He has established the united order. He established it among the people of Enoch."[2]

In our day, the Lord has decreed that at least three key characteristics must exist among the people of Zion: purity, unity, and equality. In 1833, the Lord spoke to the Prophet Joseph Smith at Kirtland about purity, saying, "Let Zion rejoice, for this is Zion—The Pure in Heart; therefore, let Zion rejoice, while all the wicked shall mourn" (D&C 97:21). In 1834, the Lord spoke again of Zion and emphasized the necessity of unity and equality: "But behold, [my people] have not learned to be obedient to the things which I required at their hands, but are full of all manner of evil, and do not impart of their substance, as becometh saints, to the poor and afflicted among them; And are not united according to the union required by the law of the celestial kingdom; And Zion cannot be built up unless it is by the principles of the law of the celestial kingdom; otherwise I cannot receive her unto myself" (D&C 105:3–5).

Elsewhere, the Lord said, "For if ye are not equal in earthly things ye cannot be equal in obtaining heavenly things" (D&C 78:6). Unity is the fundamental principle of celestial law—the principle by which the celestial kingdom operates. This helps us understand to an even greater degree why the resurrected Savior emphasized unity among the remnant of Joseph's seed in the New World.

The idea that Zion can be established on earth rests on the premise that there is a celestial prototype, a heavenly society composed of exalted beings who live in unity in God's literal presence. Zion on earth is to be patterned after that celestial society. Thus, God's desire for the ultimate destiny of a Zion community is that it be taken into his presence, for "Zion cannot be built up unless it is by the principles of the law of the celestial kingdom; *otherwise I cannot receive her unto myself*" (D&C 105:5; emphasis added).

Anciently, the people of Enoch's city molded their lives to conform with the principles of Zion and were taken unto the Lord, or translated.

> And the Lord called his people Zion, because they were of one heart and one mind, and dwelt in righteousness; and there was no poor among them. And Enoch continued his preaching in righteousness unto the people of God. And it came to pass in his days, that he built a city that was called the City of Holiness, even Zion. . . . And it came to pass that the Lord showed unto Enoch all the inhabitants of the earth; and he beheld, and lo, Zion, in process of time, was taken up into heaven. And the Lord said unto Enoch: Behold mine abode forever. (Moses 7:18–19, 21)

The same is true of Melchizedek's people. They were translated and taken to heaven: "And men having this faith, coming up unto this order of God, were translated and taken up into heaven. And now, Melchizedek was a priest of this order; therefore he obtained peace in Salem, and was called the Prince of peace. And his people wrought righteousness, and obtained heaven, and sought for the city of Enoch which God had before taken, separating it from the earth, having reserved it unto the latter days, or the end of the world" (JST, Genesis 14:32–34).

Among the remnant of Joseph in the Western Hemisphere the Lord was teaching his people how to live so as to be able to establish Zion. Fourth Nephi tells us that they achieved it. The Zion community we see emerging in 3 Nephi, and then established full-blown in 4 Nephi, was founded on teachings and practices emphasized by the Savior during his three-day sojourn.

THE CONVERSION TO CHRIST

The remarkable community of Zion described in 4 Nephi was established on the American continent sometime between the thirty-fourth and thirty-sixth year after the birth of our Lord.[3] Discipleship in Christ was the foundation of that community. All social progress and goodness centered in Jesus Christ, whose remarkable three days of personal instruction established an age of righteousness lasting 165 years. Every individual was wholly converted to the Savior—to his ideas and exemplary behavior (4 Nephi 1:2). This conversion changed the inner person through repentance (4 Nephi 1:1). Every person was thus prepared to participate in the life-giving and renewing ordinances available through the Melchizedek Priesthood, especially the gift of the Holy Ghost (4 Nephi 1:1). The people actually began to live as Jesus had taught them, and the Holy Ghost he had promised them upon his arrival elevated each of them to a new level of spirituality (3 Nephi 11:35; 12:1–2; 28:11).

A natural by-product of the constant influence and power of the Holy Ghost prevalent among the citizens of this society was the desire on the part of all the people to deal justly and fairly with each other. Therefore, the people had all things in common and all acts conformed to the pattern of the Savior's life. In sum, complete conversion to the Lord eliminated contention, produced unselfish self-regulation, and resulted in economic and political equality and freedom (4 Nephi 1:3).

Lack of Contention

A striking feature of Mormon's description of Zion in 4 Nephi is the total lack of contention in the land, which he mentions no less than four times (see 4 Nephi 1:2, 13, 15, 18). This was due to the complete unity of a civilization in which there were neither Nephites, "Lamanites, nor any manner of -ites," but all were one in Christ (see 4 Nephi 1:17) because the love of God dwelt in their hearts (see 4 Nephi 1:15). This is exactly what Jesus had emphasized when he sojourned among the people (3 Nephi 11:22, 28; 18:34).

Mormon was something of an expert on contention or civil strife, having read much about it in the records of Alma, Helaman, and Nephi, and having experienced it firsthand during his lifetime. The complete harmony and total unity of the people living in the society that had witnessed the Savior's visitation must have been a stunning development in Mormon's panoramic view of Nephite history.

The civil structure described in 4 Nephi displayed a total absence of destructive or divisive elements, including poverty, selfishness, and social Darwinism (survival of the fittest). This resulted in a kind of classlessness, elimination of crime, and allowance for society's resources to be applied to and focused on urban renewal:

> And the Lord did prosper them exceedingly in the land; yea, insomuch that they did build cities again where there had been cities burned.
>
> Yea, even that great city Zarahemla did they cause to be built again. . . .
>
> And there were no envyings, nor strifes, nor tumults, nor whoredoms, nor lyings, nor murders, nor any manner of lasciviousness; and surely there could not be a happier people among all the people who had been created by the hand of God.
>
> There were no robbers, nor murderers, neither were there Lamanites, nor any manner of -ites; but they were in one, the children of Christ, and heirs to the kingdom of God." (4 Nephi 1:7–8, 16–17)

Only true conversion to Christ and strict adherence to his example and teachings could bring significant renewal and reconstruction to a people whose civilization was all but destroyed at the time of the Crucifixion. Only true conversion to Christ could do more than offer mere stop-gap measures to solve social problems. President Ezra Taft Benson said: "The Lord works from the inside out. The world works from the outside in. The world would take people out of the slums. Christ takes the slums out of people, and then they take themselves out of the slums. The world would mold men by changing their environment. Christ changes men, who then change their environment. The world would shape human behavior, but Christ can change human nature."[4] Certainly the pattern of events described in 4 Nephi bears this out.

In addition to socioeconomic reform, civic rejuvenation, and urban renewal, the people of Nephi enjoyed increased health, strength, and vigor: "And now, behold, it came to pass that the people of Nephi did wax strong, and did multiply exceedingly fast, and became an exceedingly fair and delightsome people" (4 Nephi 1:10).

In the Christ-centered society reported in 4 Nephi, the people also witnessed a rich and astounding outpouring of miracles, including those that symbolized the mortal Messiah's absolute power over life and death: raising the dead. And, indicative of the Christ-centered nature of this religious society, we are told that no miracles were done "save it were in the name of Jesus" (4 Nephi 1:5).

The covenant community of Zion described in 4 Nephi was a literal fulfillment of the oft-repeated prophetic teaching throughout the Book of Mormon that if people would keep God's commandments then they would prosper in the land, seemingly in all ways. As Mormon says of the people living during the post-Resurrection and post-visitation era of 4 Nephi, "The Lord did bless them in all their doings" (4 Nephi 1:18).

PRAYER

Fervent, mighty, consistent, selfless prayer was and is essential to the establishment of Zion. Zion is founded on prayer. In fact, prayer is the wellspring from which most good things in mortality derive. As with all things, Jesus not only taught the people how to pray, but showed them how as well—repeatedly. He gave his first substantial instruction on prayer in the sermon at the temple, wherein he taught two profound truths. First, God the Father knows what things anyone needs before they supplicate him (3 Nephi 13:8 and 32). In fact, the Father knows all things, which is one reason we may have complete confidence in him. But it is also why we cannot deceive him. President Spencer W. Kimball elaborated on this in our day:

> In our prayers, there must be no glossing over, no hypocrisy, since there can here be no deception. The Lord knows our true condition. Do we tell the Lord how good we are, or how weak? We stand naked before him. Do we offer our supplications in modesty, sincerity, and with a "broken heart and contrite spirit," or like the Pharisee who prided himself on how well he adhered to the law of Moses? Do we offer a few trite words and worn-out phrases, or do we talk intimately to the Lord for as long as the occasion requires? Do we pray occasionally when we should be praying regularly, often, constantly? Do we pay the price to get answers to our prayers?[5]

The second great matter to which Jesus gave considerable attention in the sermon is the true order or pattern of prayer (3 Nephi 13:9–13). That he intended his sample prayer, what has come to be known as the "Lord's Prayer," as only a pattern and not as a prescribed recitation is clear from his instruction, *"After this manner* therefore pray ye" (3 Nephi 13:9; emphasis added). Jesus instructed his disciples to pray to the Father, teaching them that the Father's name is to be hallowed or sanctified, and that God presides over his kingdom and possess *all* power (3 Nephi 13:9, 13). God the Father and God the Son deserve our profoundest respect: "let all men beware how they take my name in their lips" said the Lord (D&C 63:61).

Both the New Testament Gospels and 3 Nephi indicate that Jesus often went off by himself to pray. On the second day he was with the multitude it was recorded:

> And it came to pass that Jesus departed out of the midst of them, and went a little way off from them and bowed himself to the earth, and he said:
> Father, I thank thee that thou hast given the Holy Ghost unto these whom I have chosen; and it is because of their belief in me that I have chosen them out of the world. . . .
> And it came to pass that when Jesus had thus prayed unto the Father, he came unto his disciples, and behold, they did still continue, without ceasing, to pray unto him; and they did not multiply many words, for it was given unto them what they should pray, and they were filled with desire. (3 Nephi 19:19–20, 22–24)

Here we also see that many words do not make mighty prayers. Rather, as Elder Bruce R. McConkie pointed out, "Perfect prayers are those which are inspired, in which the Spirit reveals the words which should be used."[6] In this vein, the Lord declared, "And if ye are purified and cleansed from all sin, ye shall ask whatsoever you will in the name of Jesus and it shall be done. But know this, it shall be given you what you shall ask" (D&C 50:29–30). Thus, as Nephi recorded, "it was given unto them what they should pray" (3 Nephi 19:24). Jesus offered inspired prayers, and this influenced his disciples to do the same.

The power and content of Jesus's personal prayers deeply affected the people. Consider this episode:

> And he turned from them again, and went a little way off and bowed himself to the earth; and he prayed again unto the Father, saying:
>
> Father, I thank thee that thou hast purified those whom I have chosen, because of their faith, and I pray for them, and also for them who shall believe on their words, that they may be purified in me, through faith on their words, even as they are purified in me.
>
> Father, I pray not for the world, but for those whom thou hast given me out of the world, because of their faith, that they may be purified in me, that I may be in them as thou, Father, art in me, that we may be one, that I may be glorified in them.
>
> And when Jesus had spoken these words he came again unto his disciples; and behold they did pray steadfastly, without ceasing, unto him; and he did smile upon them again; and behold they were white, even as Jesus.
>
> And it came to pass that he went again a little way off and prayed unto the Father;
>
> And tongue cannot speak the words which he prayed, neither can be written by man the words which he prayed.
>
> And the multitude did hear and do bear record; and their hearts were open and they did understand in their hearts the words which he prayed.
>
> Nevertheless, so great and marvelous were the words which he prayed that they cannot be written, neither can they be uttered by man. (3 Nephi 19:27–34)

Hearing Jesus pray caused the multitude to have their hearts opened, and to understand by the Holy Spirit the thoughts and intents of the Savior's heart. We also see a distinct parallel between this prayer and Jesus's Great High Priestly petition offered in the Old World. Compare, for example, 3 Nephi 19:29 with John 17:6.

> Father, I pray not for the world, but for those whom thou hast given me out of the world, because of their faith, that they may be purified in me, that I may be in them as thou, Father, art in me, that we may be one, that I may be glorified in them. (3 Nephi 19:29)

> I have manifested thy name unto the men which thou gavest me out of the world: thine they were, and thou gavest them me; and they have kept thy word. . . . I pray for them: I pray not for the world, but for them which thou hast given me; for they are thine. . . . That they all may be one; as thou, Father, art in me, and I in thee, that they also may be one in us: that the world may believe that thou hast sent me. (John 17:6, 9, 21)

Not surprisingly, Jesus commanded the people to "pray always," especially to avoid the snares of the devil (3 Nephi 18:15–19). Family prayer was and is a powerful protection and guiding influence for disciples of Jesus. President Gordon B. Hinckley indicated how fathers, mothers, and children are blessed through family prayer:

> I feel satisfied that there is no adequate substitute for the morning and evening practice of kneeling together—father, mother, and children. This, more than soft carpets, more than lovely draperies, more than cleverly balanced color schemes, is the thing that will make for better and more beautiful homes. . . .
> I know of no better way to inculcate love for country than for parents to pray before their children for the land in which they live, invoking the blessings of the Almighty upon it that it may be preserved in liberty and in peace. I know of no better way than to build within the hearts of our children a much-needed respect for authority than remembering in the daily supplications of the family the leaders of our respective countries who carry the burdens of government. . . .
> I know of nothing that will so much help to ease family tensions, that in a subtle way will bring about the respect for parents which leads to obedience, that will affect the spirit of repentance which will largely erase the blight of broken homes, than will praying together, confessing weaknesses together before the Lord, and invoking the blessings of the Lord upon the home and those who dwell there.[7]

Jesus knew that no greater activity could be engaged in to bring about Zion than consistent family prayer. Every aspect of society would be improved through family prayer, as President Hinckley again testified: "This practice, a return to family worship, spreading across the land and over the earth, would in a generation largely lift the blight that is destroying us. It would restore integrity, mutual respect, and a spirit of thankfulness in the hearts of people." [8]

Third Nephi also records that on one occasion Jesus "commanded the multitude that they should cease to pray." But he also commanded them that they should not cease to pray in their hearts" (3 Nephi 20:1). This is valuable, indeed indispensible, counsel to have preserved for modern disciples.

Of more than passing interest in 3 Nephi is the instance when the multitude prayed directly to Jesus (3 Nephi 19:18, 25, 30), which seems to contradict the Savior's own instruction that the faithful should pray unto the Father in his name (3 Nephi 13:9; 18:23; 19:7–8). Two thoughts occur. First, it is possible that this prayer was done more in the sense of praising and worshipping Jesus than participating in the regular pattern of prayer. The people were, after all, standing in the presence of God! That Jesus did not forbid them is a telling indicator that their action was acceptable. Second, the multitude may also have prayed to Jesus having God the Father in mind as well. Elder Bruce R. McConkie indicated as much: "Jesus was present before them as the symbol of the Father. Seeing him, it was as though they saw the Father; praying to him, it was as though they prayed to the Father. It was a special and unique situation that as far as we know has taken place only once on earth during all the long ages of the Lord's hand-dealings with his children." [9]

SACRAMENT

Worthy participation in the sacrament of the Lord's Supper on a regular basis was another foundational principle on which Zion was established in the Western Hemisphere. Moroni's abridged history of society after the Savior's three-day ministry implies this: "And they did not walk any more after the performances and ordinances of the law of Moses; but they did walk after the commandments which they had received from their Lord and their God, continuing in fasting and prayer, and in meeting together oft both to pray and to hear the word of the Lord" (4 Nephi 1:12).

The old performances of the law of Moses were fulfilled. The new ordinance, the sacrament, replaced animal sacrifice and pointed to the new required offering of a broken heart and contrite spirit (3 Nephi 9:19–20). Animal sacrifice was rich in symbolism, pointing *forward* to the atoning sacrifice of Jesus Christ. The sacrament is also rich in symbolism, pointing *back* to the bodily sacrifice of the Son of God—the great and last sacrifice (Alma 34:13–14). Elder McConkie explained:

> As sacrifice was thus to cease with the occurrence of the great event toward which it pointed, there must needs be a new ordinance to replace it, an ordinance which also would center the attention of the saints on the infinite and eternal atonement. And so Jesus . . . initiated the sacrament of the Lord's Supper. Sacrifice stopped and sacrament started. It was the end of the old era, the beginning of the new. Sacrifice looked forward to the shed blood and bruised flesh of the Lamb of God. The sacrament was to be in remembrance of his spilt blood and broken flesh, the emblems, bread and wine, typifying such as completely as had the shedding of the blood of animals in their days.[10]

Jesus introduced the sacrament to Joseph's remnant on the first day of his visit (3 Nephi 18:1–13). On that occasion, he administered the ordinance to the Twelve, who in turn administered it to the multitude. When all "had eaten and were filled" (3 Nephi 18:5), he taught them the doctrinal significance of what they were doing. They partook of the bread to remember the Bread of Life, or as he said, "This shall ye do in remembrance of my body, which I have shown unto you" (3 Nephi 18:7). This statement would have been so powerful to the multitude, and provided such a graphic illustration, precisely because they had just felt the prints of the nails in his hands, feet, and side only hours before (3 Nephi 11:14–15). In our day it is also important to realize that by remembering the Savior's bruised and broken body in Gethsemane and on the Cross, we have the promise that our bodies will be raised up to eternal life.

Jesus commanded the twelve disciples that the sanctity of the sacrament was to be carefully guarded. He said to them, "This is the commandment which I give unto you, that ye shall not suffer any one knowingly to partake of my flesh and blood unworthily, when ye shall minister it (3 Nephi 18:28). Jesus imposed a heavy penalty on those who partake of the sacrament unworthily—"damnation to his soul" (3 Nephi 18:29). Therefore, those who administered the sacrament were to forbid such a person from partaking of it. Nevertheless, said the Savior, that person was not to be cast out of their midst but was to be ministered unto and nourished spiritually, to be helped in the repentance process, and then to be given access to the ordinances. The Lord emphasized this point in such a way so as to let ancient and modern disciples know that he truly cares about sinners and the downtrodden. Such an attitude is the essence of living in a Zion community. Jesus's words on this point are both thought-provoking and humbling: "Ye shall not cast him out of your synagogues, or your places of worship, for unto such shall ye continue to minister; for ye know not but what they will return and repent, and come unto me with full purpose of heart, and I shall heal them; and ye shall be the means of bringing salvation unto them" (3 Nephi 18:32).

Another implication is clear: Zion cannot be achieved without repentance. The great patriarch Melchizedek, for example, ministered unto the vilest of sinners. He "was a king over the land of Salem; and his people had waxed strong in iniquity and abomination; yea, they had all gone astray; they were full of all manner of wickedness" (Alma 13:17). But Melchizedek exercised such mighty faith and priesthood power among his people that they not only repented but established Zion in their day and were translated just like the City of Enoch (JST, Genesis 14:32–34).

The importance of the sacrament in the Lord's view is shown by the number of times it was prepared and passed during the three days Jesus was with the people. It was inaugurated on the first day (3 Nephi 18:1–11) and it was administered again on the second day (3 Nephi 20:3–9). And after the end of his three day visit, Jesus "did show himself unto them oft, and did break bread oft, and bless it, and give it unto them" (3 Nephi 26:13). Jesus told his followers that if they would "always do these things" they would be blessed and "built upon my rock" (3 Nephi 18: 12). This is a great promise in mortality. The sacrament keeps disciples on the path to perfection. It motivates all followers of the Savior to think deeply about him, to be like him, and to live in such a way that they can enjoy the environment of heaven on earth, or in other words, experience Zion as the ancients did. No wonder Jesus commanded his people to partake of the sacrament often.

THE COVENANT

The Savior taught his American Israelites that they were of the lineage of Abraham, the "father of the faithful" (D&C 138:41). As his "seed" they were entitled to the blessings promised to their forefathers by God through the covenant entered into by both parties (Genesis 17:2, 7). The Lord said to them: "And behold, ye are the children of the prophets; and ye are of the house of Israel; and ye are of the covenant which the Father made with your fathers, saying unto Abraham: and in thy seed shall all the kindreds of the earth be blessed" (3 Nephi 20:25).

The promises of the Abrahamic covenant include, but are not limited to

1. promised land (Abraham 2:6; Genesis 17:8);
2. numerous posterity (Abraham 2:9; Genesis 17:4–5);
3. priesthood power and authority (Abraham 2:9,10);
4. salvation (Abraham 2:11).

The Savior emphasized that the blessings of the covenant could only be realized by righteous living. That is why he told the people that the Father had sent him to them in the New World: "The Father having raised me up unto you first, and sent me to bless you in turning away every one of you from his iniquities; and this because ye are the children of the covenant" (3 Nephi 20:26)." The Savior also indicated that the promised blessings associated with the Abrahamic covenant were beginning to be fulfilled by giving to them their land of promise: "And the Father hath commanded me that I should give unto you this land, for your inheritance" (3 Nephi 20:14).

The gathering of Abraham's children occurs in two ways, according to the Savior. First, they are gathered to their promised lands, and second, they are gathered to a knowledge of God through the holy priesthood, especially in the Lord's temples. In June of 1843, the Prophet Joseph Smith elaborated upon the connection between the gathering of God's people and temples. He said: "What was the object of gathering the Jews, or the people of God in any age of the world? . . . The main object was to build unto the Lord a house whereby He could reveal unto His people the ordinances of His house and the glories of His kingdom, and teach the people the way of salvation; for there are certain ordinances and principles that, when they are taught and practiced, must be done in a place or a house built for that purpose." [11]

In another revelation given in 1838, now known as Doctrine and Covenants 124, the Lord said that he intended for temples to be built among his people in every age. He commanded Moses, for example,

That he should build a tabernacle, that they should bear it with them in the wilderness, and to build a house in the land of promise, that those ordinances might be revealed which had been hid from before the world was. . . . [F]or the beginning of revelations and foundation of Zion and for the glory, honor, and endowment of all her municipals . . . by the ordinance of my holy house, which my people are always commanded to build unto my holy name. (D&C 124:38–39)

Thus, the establishment of Zion is an outgrowth of the Abrahamic covenant, the gathering of God's people to their lands of inheritance, and the building of temples where sacred information, power, and ordinances are bestowed. The Zion community emerging in 3 Nephi and described in greater detail in 4 Nephi was built upon these principles and developments.

Two other matters are important to acknowledge and appreciate. First is the role of the Father in the fulfillment of the Abrahamic covenant and the gathering together of Abraham's posterity. Second is the fact that the Abrahamic covenant was not given for the house of Israel only, or any other specific branch of Abraham's family. The Abrahamic covenant is the same as the gospel and its attendant covenants (Abraham 2:10). The blessings of the Abrahamic covenant—the blessings of the Gospel—are intended for everyone, including the gentiles. As the Savior said to the remnant of Joseph in the land of Bountiful, "And after that ye were blessed then fulfilleth the Father the covenant which he made with Abraham, saying: In thy seed shall all the kindreds of the earth be blessed—unto the pouring out of the Holy Ghost through me upon the Gentiles, which blessing upon the Gentiles shall make them mighty above all" (3 Nephi 20:27).

In fact, it was the wisdom and will of the Father, that the Gentiles should be established in America, "and be set up as a free people by the power of the Father, that these things might come forth from them unto a remnant of your seed, that the covenant of the Father may be fulfilled which he had covenanted with his people, O house of Israel" (3 Nephi 21:4). The things to come forth, mentioned in this verse, included the Book of Mormon and the Prophet Joseph Smith, of whom Jesus also prophesied as he addressed the multitude (3 Nephi 20:7–11).

The Savior went on to quote Isaiah 54 to the multitude to assure them that all of the things he had said would come to pass. Zion and her stakes would indeed be established in the last days, and all of the house of Israel would be gathered through the mercy and tenderness of God, and would triumph in the end (3 Nephi 22).

SOME FINAL TEACHINGS

As mentioned, during his three days of instruction Jesus quoted several passages of scripture to his New World Israelites. This followed his well-established pattern in the Old World, and suggests to modern readers the divinely approved method for teaching in the kingdom of God in any age.

Included in Jesus's carefully selected passages from Malachi was the well-known commandment for God's people to tithe all their increase. Most modern readers remember this instruction well—"Will a man rob God? Yet ye have robbed me. . . . In tithes and offerings. . . . (3 Nephi 24:8; compare Malachi 3:8–10). But do we remember the magnificent promise? It surely must have inspired the multitude who stood before the Savior, a multitude who had seen their share of warfare, famine, and natural disasters of unimaginable proportions. This promise still possesses great power to inspire and motivate: "And I will rebuke the devourer for your sakes, and he shall not destroy the fruits of your ground; neither shall your vine cast her fruit before the time in the fields, saith the Lord of Hosts. And all nations shall call you blessed, for ye shall be a delightsome land, saith the Lord of Hosts" (3 Nephi 24:11–12).

As it did anciently, the doctrine of tithes and offerings constitutes one of the foundation stones upon which Zion is built in modern times. Those who observe it shall be counted as the Lord's in that day when he comes to "make up [his] jewels," and he will "spare them as a man spareth his own son that serveth him" (3 Nephi 24:17).

CONCLUSION

As the Savior's time with his New World disciples drew to a close, he delivered his Gospel defining discourse recorded in 3 Nephi 27 (see chapter six herein), and afterward he expressed his joy over what had transpired during his time with the people. He then made them a truly extraordinary promise: "And now I go unto the Father. And verily I say unto you, whatsoever things ye shall ask the Father in my name shall be given unto you. . . . And now, behold, my joy is great, even unto fulness, because of you, and also this generation; yea, and even the Father rejoiceth, and also all the holy angels, because of you and this generation; for none of them are lost" (3 Nephi 27:28, 30).

Indeed, the Savior did have great reason to rejoice. The Zion society he had been preparing Joseph's remnant to establish was realized. The Savior's appearance, visitation, and instruction by precept and example changed a people and the world. If these developments had to be reduced to a single concept, I have to believe that ultimately it was the people's response to a solitary exhortation that made all the difference: "Therefore, what manner of men ought ye to be? Verily I say unto you, even as I am" (3 Nephi 27:27). And they were!

From start to finish, 3 Nephi is magnificent. Like the other Gospels, this Fifth Gospel begins with the Savior's birth. It ends, as Elder Jeffrey R. Holland reminds us, "with the fundamental declaration that he [Jesus] had come into the world to do the will of the Father," [12] and with the exhortation to all of his followers to do likewise (3 Nephi 27:27). Third Nephi is a primer on "the Gospel"—what it is and why it matters. It emphasizes a profound concept—that where Christ's Gospel is concerned it is all a matter of "will," whether we choose to follow God's or our own. This is the heart of the issue. The former way leads to glory; the latter to misery. The former way guarantees us the infinite help of God; the latter leaves us on our own. The former way is truly good news.

My reading again of the Fifth Gospel has convinced me that it has more nuggets to offer than can possibly be mined in one short volume like this one—or even a lifetime of investigation. Therefore, it is truly arresting to think that this Fifth Gospel records only a small portion of what Jesus Christ said and did in the New World. In fact, according to its own testimony, it does not even present "a hundredth part of the teachings which Jesus did truly teach unto the people" (3 Nephi 26:6). In this regard, it sounds very much like the Gospel of John, which lamented that "there are also many other things which Jesus did, the which, if they should be written everyone . . . even the world itself could not contain the books that should be written" (John 21:25).

And as magnificent as the Gospel of John truly is, or the other three for that matter, still, to me, the Fifth Gospel stands above all of them. Nothing quite like the Savior's three-day visit to the Western Hemisphere appears in world literature. It could be argued, I suppose, that the forty-day post-Resurrection ministry of Jesus Christ, recorded in the New Testament, is of the same genre. But even here only bits and pieces have come to us. The Fifth Gospel is unparalleled.

The late Professor Hugh Nibley has ably captured our feelings about the remarkable ministry of Jesus Christ in the New World:

> The comings and goings of the Savior moving between heaven and earth are charged with excitement. As mortals dealing with the mundane, we wonder whether such things can really be. . . . The wonder of it quickens the reader's pulse, but how could we describe the state of mind of those who actually experienced it? The early day Christian writings try, but it is 3 Nephi 19:1–3 that really catches the emotion. In 3 Nephi we see the celestial splendor of his comings and goings. We see the utter glory of his presence. And we see the Savior's closest and most loving intimacy, which is especially tender in the accounts of his dealings with children.
>
> And so, we may well ask, "What imposter with no text or precedent to guide him could hope to venture into the unexplored morass of the Old World forty-day accounts where to this day the student finds no solid foothold, without quickly coming to grief?" The calm, unhesitating deliberation with which the author of 3 Nephi proceeds where religious scholars and poets have feared to tread has been explained as an example of Joseph Smith's impudence—a desperate argument. The other explanation—that he was translating an authentic document—deserves a fair hearing.[13]

In the end, it is the Fifth Gospel that holds us spellbound. It is the Fifth Gospel that gives the other Gospel accounts true meaning and credibility. In fact, the Fifth Gospel serves as a bridge between the first half of the New Testament (the Gospels) and the second half (Acts through Revelation). It is the Fifth Gospel that constitutes the capstone of ancient testimonies of the Father and the Son *working in tandem* through priesthood leaders to bring about "the immortality and eternal life of man" (Moses 1:39). In modern times the Savior referred to the Book of Mormon as his "new covenant" with the house of Israel (D&C 84:57). Indeed, the Fifth Gospel is a tangible witness of the Father's and the Son's culminating covenant with all humankind (see 3 Nephi 21:1; 29: chapter heading). In the end, the Fifth Gospel is a gift of lasting, even eternal, value to all humankind.

NOTES

1. Joseph Smith, *Teachings of the Prophet Joseph Smith*, sel. Joseph Fielding Smith (Salt Lake City: Deseret Book, 1977), 160.

2. Marion G. Romney, "The Purpose of Church Welfare Services," *Ensign*, May 1977, 92.

3. The commonly accepted dates of AD 34 and 36 that are associated with the beginning of 4 Nephi rest on the Book of Mormon dating of Christ's birth as being 1 BC.

4. Ezra Taft Benson, "Born of God," *Ensign*, November 1985, 6.

5. Spencer W. Kimball, *Faith Precedes the Miracle* (Salt Lake City: Deseret Book, 1972), 207.

6. Bruce R. McConkie, *Mormon Doctrine* (Salt Lake City: Bookcraft, 1966), 586.

7. Gordon B. Hinckley, "The Blessings of Family Prayer," *Ensign*, February 1991, 2–5.

8. Ibid., 5.

9. Bruce R. McConkie, *The Promised Messiah* (Salt Lake City: Deseret Book, 1978), 561.

10. Bruce R. McConkie, *Doctrinal New Testament Commentary*, 3 vols. (Salt Lake City: Bookcraft, 1965–1971), 1:719–720.

11. Smith, *Teachings of the Prophet Joseph Smith*, 307–308.

12. Jeffrey R. Holland, *Christ and the New Covenant* (Deseret Book, 1997), 303.

13. Hugh W. Nibley, "Christ Among the Ruins," *Ensign*, July 1983, 19.

Acknowledgments

I THANK MY WIFE, JANET, FOR HER KINDNESS AND HELP IN FINISHING this manuscript, as well as my secretary, Connie Brace, for her help and superb skills. I also thank the kind and competent staff at Cedar Fort, Inc., especially Jennifer Fielding and Emily Chambers, for bringing my thoughts to fruition.

About the Author

Andrew C. Skinner is a former dean of Religious Education (2000–2005) at Brigham Young University, Provo, Utah, and former executive director of the Neal A. Maxwell Institute for Religious Scholarship at BYU (2005–2008). In Fall 2010, he was appointed Richard L. Evans Professor of Religious Understanding. He is a professor of ancient scripture and Near Eastern studies, a member of the international editorial group that worked on the Dead Sea Scrolls, and the author, coauthor, or editor of twenty books and over two hundred articles on religious and historical topics. He is a graduate of the University of Colorado, holds master's degrees from Iliff School of Theology and Harvard University in Hebrew Bible and Judaic studies, and has a PhD in European and Near Eastern history from the University of Denver. He pursued graduate studies at Hebrew University in Jerusalem, taught at BYU's Jerusalem Center for Near Eastern studies on several occasions, and served there as Associate Director for Academics, most recently from August through December 2011. Brother Skinner has served in various callings in the LDS Church, including bishop, a member of the Church's Correlation Evaluation Committee, and a member of the Sunday School General Board. He is married to Janet Corbridge Skinner, and they are the parents of six children.